PSYCHOANALYSIS, INTERNATIONAL RELATIONS, AND DIPLOMACY

PSYCHOANALYSIS, INTERNATIONAL RELATIONS, AND DIPLOMACY

A Sourcebook on Large-Group Psychology

Vamık D. Volkan

Routledge
Taylor & Francis Group

LONDON AND NEW YORK

First published 2014 by Karnac Books Ltd.

Published 2018 by Routledge
2 Park Square, Milton Park, Abingdon, Oxon OX14 4RN
711 Third Avenue, New York, NY 10017, USA

Routledge is an imprint of the Taylor & Francis Group, an informa business

British Library Cataloguing in Publication Data

A C.I.P. for this book is available from the British Library

ISBN-13: 9781782201250 (pbk)

Typeset by V Publishing Solutions Pvt Ltd., Chennai, India

CONTENTS

ABOUT THE AUTHOR   vii

FOREWORD
Psychoanalysis and political conflict: is psychoanalysis relevant?   ix
Howard B. Levine

ABOUT THIS BOOK   xvii

CHAPTER ONE
Diplomats and psychoanalysts   1

CHAPTER TWO
Large-group identity, shared prejudice, chosen glories, and chosen
    traumas   17

CHAPTER THREE
Entitlement ideologies   33

CHAPTER FOUR
The Crusades, the fall of Constantinople, and the "Megali Idea"   39

CHAPTER FIVE
Traumatised large groups, societal shifts, and transgenerational
    transmissions   45

CHAPTER SIX
Large-group regression and progression   59

CHAPTER SEVEN
Unending mourning and memorials   65

CHAPTER EIGHT
Political leaders' personalities   77

CHAPTER NINE
Reactivation of a chosen trauma   89

CHAPTER TEN
Intertwining old "memories" and affects with current ones   103

CHAPTER ELEVEN
Political propaganda, suicide bombers, and terrorism   109

CHAPTER TWELVE
"Unofficial" diplomacy and psychoanalytic
    large-group psychology   121

REFERENCES   129

INDEX   143

ABOUT THE AUTHOR

Vamık Volkan is an Emeritus Professor of Psychiatry at the University of Virginia, Charlottesville, Virginia; the Senior Erik Erikson Scholar at the Erikson Institute of Education and Research of the Austen Riggs Center, Stockbridge, Massachusetts; and an Emeritus Training and Supervising Analyst at the Washington Psychoanalytic Institute, Washington, D.C. He served as the Medical Director of the University of Virginia's Blue Ridge Hospital and as director of the University of Virginia's Center for the Study of Mind and Human Interaction (CSMHI). He was a member of the International Negotiation Network under the directorship of the former President Jimmy Carter; an Inaugural Yitzhak Rabin Fellow, Rabin Center for Israeli Studies, Tel Aviv, Israel; and a Fulbright/Sigmund-Freud-Privatstiftung Visiting Scholar of Psychoanalysis and a Visiting Professor of Political Science, the University of Vienna, Vienna, Austria. He received the Sigmund Freud Award given by the city of Vienna in collaboration with the World Council of Psychotherapy. He holds Honorary Doctorate degrees from Kuopio University, Finland and from Ankara University, Turkey. He is a former President of the *Turkish-American Neuropsychiatric Society*, the *International Society of Political Psychology (ISPP)*, the

Virginia Psychoanalytic Society and the *American College of Psychoanalysts.* He is the author, co-author, editor, or co-editor of dozens of books and the author of hundreds of book chapters and academic papers. He has served on the editorial boards of sixteen professional journals including *the Journal of the American Psychoanalytic Association.*

Psychoanalysis and political conflict: is psychoanalysis relevant?*

Psychoanalysis occupies a marginalised position in regard to international diplomacy and world conflict. Because its principle areas of study include the unconscious forces that shape human motivation, and their roots in aggression and desire, it was once assumed that familiarity with the unconscious and the destructive tendencies inherent in human nature might offer analysts a unique and privileged position from which to understand and attempt to contribute to the resolution of national and international crises.

In the aftermath of World War I, for example, the International Institute of Intellectual Co-operation, instructed by the Permanent Committee for Literature and the Arts of the League of Nations, asked Einstein to engage with Freud (1933b) in a correspondence aimed at exploring whether human nature made war inevitable. Noting that "the history

---

*Portions of this essay appeared in a previous publication, Levine, H. B. (2006). Large-group dynamics and world conflict: The contributions of Vamık Volkan: "Blood Lines: From Ethnic Pride to Ethnic Terrorism." By Vamık Volkan. New York: Farrar, Straus & Giroux, 1997, 280 pp., $19.00. "Blind Trust: Large Groups and Their Leaders in Times of Crisis and Terror." By Vamık Volkan. Charlottesville, VA: Pitchstone, 2004, 367 pp., $19.95. *Journal of the American Psychoanalytic Association*, 54: 273–280.

of the human race reveals an endless series of conflicts between one community and another or several others, between larger and smaller units—between cities, provinces, races, nations, empires—which have almost always been settled by force of arms" (p. 207), Freud implicated the innate destructiveness of the death instinct in any explanation of man's bellicosity—that is, it is inherent in mankind's *nature* to be aggressive, cruel, and destructive—but also acknowledged that this view was perhaps too distant from immediate experience to be of practical use: "The result [i.e., Freud's response to Einstein's inquiry] … is not very fruitful when an unworldly theoretician is called in to advise on an urgent practical problem" (p. 213).

Years earlier, faced with the cataclysmic devastation that was beginning to be unleashed in the First World War, which had broken out six months earlier, Freud (1915b) wrote an essay on "The Disillusionment of War". There, he reflected on the fact that despite the close tie between civilisation, culture, and morality, a tie that one might hope or suspect would produce a feeling of unity and community among people of all nations, a war had broken out that was, if anything, "more bloody and more destructive than any war of other days … at least as cruel, as embittered, as implacable as any that has preceded it" (p. 278).

How was this to be explained? How could it have come about that despite the enormous cultural contributions and advances of Western society (particularly Germanic Western society) a war was loosed that in Freud's words:

> tramples in blind fury on all that comes in its way, as though there were to be no future and no peace among men after it is over. It cuts all the common bonds between the contending peoples, and threatens to leave a legacy of embitterment that will make any reversal of those bonds impossible for a long time to come. (Freud, 1915b, p. 279)

While Freud's understanding of this phenomenon was powerful for its time—he identified the conflict as existing between the ethical advances of culture and society that tried, often unsuccessfully, to keep the abiding primitive impulses that all are subject to at bay—it was limited in detail and specificity.

On the one hand, he noted that:

> the influences of civilization cause an ever increasing transformation of egoistic trends into altruistic and social ones. (p. 282)

On the other hand, he recognised, that:

> when the community no longer raises objections [to "brutal and arbitrary conduct"], there is an end ... to the suppression of evil passions, and men perpetrate deeds of cruelty, fraud, treachery, and barbarity so incompatible with their level of civilization that one would have thought them impossible. (p. 280)

This acknowledgment of the fragility of society's restraints echoed the concerns of "warning voices, which declared that old traditional differences made wars inevitable" (p. 278) and reflected the hard fact of how impotent logical arguments may be against affective interests (p. 287).

Freud reluctantly concluded that:

> nations obey their passions far more readily than their interests ... [It remained] a mystery why the collective individuals should in fact despise, hate and detest one another—every nation against every other—and even in times of peace ... It is just as though when it becomes a question of a number of people, not to say millions, all individual moral acquisitions are obliterated, and only the most primitive, the oldest, the crudest mental attitudes are left. (p. 288)

Put in contemporary terms, we might resignedly say that the voice of reason and the subtleties of psychoanalytic thinking hold little sway before the forces of *realpolitik* and the inherently bellicose and destructive nature of mankind.

In the years that followed, and faced with the horrors perpetrated by one group against another in the past century, we must regrettably conclude that despite the pioneering work on small group dynamics by Freud, Bion, and others, the explanatory power of analytic theories and the clinical data on which analytic expertise is based have proven more relevant to understanding individual and dyadic behaviour and emotional development than to understanding experience and behaviour in large social groups. Attempts to apply psychoanalytic insights to politics, large social groups and the interactions between large groups and their leaders have met with little success. As a result, the ethnic, religious and cultural conflicts that have become such pervasive facts of political life in the twenty-first century have generally proven to be beyond the expertise and experience of most psychoanalysts.

In contrast to most psychoanalysts, however, Vamık Volkan, has had extensive first-hand experience working with diplomats, administrators, statesmen and other mental health professionals in the study and/ or attempted resolution of major conflicts in many of the major trouble spots of the world. Under the auspices of the Center for the Study of Mind and Human Interaction at the University of Virginia School of Medicine, which he founded and led, he has participated in the study and attempted resolution of national and international conflicts and crises and worked with politicians and intellectual leaders in Israel, Egypt, and Palestine; Soviet Union, Turkey, and Greece; Kuwait, Croatia, and Bosnia; South Ossetia and the Republic of Georgia; Latvia, Lithuania, Estonia, and Russia; Albania; Waco, Texas; etc.

As a result, the ideas and observations that he has shared across a professional lifetime (e.g., Volkan, 1997, 2004, 2013) forge a vital link between psychology and political science, as they argue persuasively for including a psychological, particularly an *unconscious* psycho-analytic psychological, dimension into any understanding of ethnic, national and international conflict. His work offers readers the outlines of a sophisticated, psychoanalytically informed theory of large group dynamics, the concepts needed to understand the relationship and interplay between individual and large-group identity, and numerous vivid and compelling illustrations drawn from contemporary world events.

Considering his professional roots as a clinical psychoanalyst, it is not surprising that Volkan's experience leads him to conclude that long standing national and ethnic conflicts:

> cannot be understood by focusing only on real-world factors, such as economic, military, legal, and political circumstances. Real-world issues are highly "psychologized"—contaminated with shared perceptions, thoughts, fantasies, and emotions (both conscious and unconscious) pertaining to past historical glories and traumas: losses, humiliations, mourning difficulties, feelings of entitlement to revenge, and resistance to accepting changed realities. (Volkan, 1997, p. 117)

He has argued persuasively that without some application of the principles of psychoanalysis, diplomats and political scientists cannot understand the full range of conscious and unconscious meanings— and the passions associated with these meanings—that individuals assign to cultural identity and ethnic attachment. The urgency to arrive at this understanding follows from the fact that it is precisely these passions and meanings that underlie religious fundamentalism, terrorism, suicide bombings, ethnic and religious conflict, ethnic violence and ethnic cleansing, each of which are subjects that he has examined and reported on in detail.

Ultimately, Volkan provides readers with a psychoanalytic theory of large-group dynamics based upon an understanding and study of the emotional bonds of large social groups, the dynamics and interaction of large groups and their leaders, and the psychology and vicissitudes of large-group identity and its relationship to individual identity. Of particular interest are his descriptions of how identity at the personal and group levels is maintained, protected, and repaired, the effects of regression on large groups under threat and how political leaders may manipulate this regression and the rituals of large-group cohesion so as to produce "an atmosphere ripe for unspeakable, seemingly inhumane acts of violence" (Volkan, 2004, p. 14).

Volkan's goal is to provide statesmen and politicians, as well as psychoanalysts and other mental health practitioners, with the conceptual tools with which to think about and begin to address some of the most pressing issues of our times. These include an understanding of:

1. "why bloody wars between neighbors not only persist, but proliferate" (Volkan, 1997, p. 20)
2. "how certain *universal* elements of human nature converge to create an atmosphere that both gives rise to violent aggressive acts, such as the September 11 attacks or war, and allows the smothering of individual rights and freedom ..." (Volkan, 2004, p. 11).

Volkan has argued that in the course of development core individual identity at the pre-Oedipal level and large-group identity become inextricably intertwined. Threats or damage to the one may have important consequences for the other. The link between the two is often outside of conscious awareness, unless one or the other is threatened, or until an event occurs in which large-group belonging evokes pleasure, anger or pain. Individuals may cling to their large-group identity as a kind of reparative "patch" for a damaged or traumatised self and the dynamic interaction between individual and large-group identity can prove central to understanding regression and violence in large-group conflicts, such as racism, ethnic and religious wars, terrorism, the recruitment and development of suicide bombers, and the psychology of large-group leadership.

Of particular interest are the positive uses to which ritual, historical meaning, and large group markers of identity—for example, *chosen traumas* and *chosen glories*—have been put, as well as their function in situations of trauma and stress that cause individual and large-group regression.

> As long as the rituals that serve to separate groups are not rigidi-fied by large-group regression, they function positively to protect and enhance large-group identity and to keep expressions of each group's aggression under control. When the tension between the competitive groups increases, however, each group's existing ritu-als of self-definition grow less flexible, and new rituals develop: rit-uals in which we can detect signs of magical thinking and blurred reality. The enemy ... [they may be] increasingly perceived as a con-glomeration of every undesirable quality; in such negative stere-otyping, the enemy is often thought of as a lower class of human, and, at worst, as actually less than human. (Volkan, 2004, p. 107)

Thus, large-group regressions may be benign or malignant, depending upon the particular social, political and historical context in which the regression occurs and the response of group members and leaders to the regression.

> When large groups are threatened by conflict, members of the group cling ever more stubbornly to ... [experiences of ethnicity, national-ity, religion and other large group affiliations] in an effort to main-tain and regulate their sense of self and their sense of belonging to a large group. At such times, large group processes become dominant and large group identity issues and rituals are more susceptible to political propaganda and manipulation. (Volkan, 2004, p. 262)

Under conditions of actual or threatened large-group regression, it is the nature of group leadership that often proves decisive to the out-come. At such times,

> basic trust of the group members may become shaken, even per-verted by the manipulation of political leaders and replaced by a

blind trust, in which leaders' views and directions are followed at
all costs and contrary to more reasonable considerations. (Volkan,
2004, pp. 13–14)

It is then that group members "will tolerate extreme shared sadism
and/or masochism in defense of the group's identity" (Volkan, 2004,
p. 133).

At its most pernicious, group leadership, often in the service of supporting the leader's own political ambitions and conscious and unconscious psychological needs, can encourage a process of demonisation and
dehumanisation of the group's enemies. This may "set the stage for terrorism, war-like conditions, and wars ..." (Volkan, 2004, pp. 107–108).

> Alternatively, it may lead to a readiness amongst group members
> to destroy themselves, "(whether in a suicide bomber's attack or a
> group's mass suicide) ... as an act of assertion ... [that] emphati-
> cally separates the identity of the group willing to sacrifice them-
> selves from that of the 'others' perceived as threatening them".
> (Volkan, 2004, p. 133)

Will this understanding of the genesis and dynamics of ethnic conflict and terrorism, offer us a small but significant reason for hope and
contribute to a conceptual plan of action? As is the case in the analytic
treatment of individuals, the remediation of the sequelae of past and
ongoing injuries lies partly in forgiveness and partly in the acknowledgment and acceptance of what has happened and in mourning for
what is lost and cannot be. These are necessary precursors for taking
concrete steps towards establishing a more constructive relationship to
the external world. A case in point may be drawn from the history of
the Middle East.

In 1977, then Prime Minister of Egypt, Anwar Sadat, journeyed to
the Israeli Knesset and delivered an historic speech, in which he said
that beyond political, military, and economic considerations, there
were *psychological* barriers of suspicion, fear, rejection, and deception
that divided the Arabs and Israelis, and that these were responsible
for seventy per cent of the problems that existed between them. This
speech, which was an important starting point for Volkan's career as
a psychopolitical observer and participant in world affairs, contains a
lesson that remains of vital importance for psychoanalysis and for the

world. Sadat's observation challenged Volkan—and should challenge us all—to wonder:

> Are there ways to apply psychoanalytically informed insights to political, legal, economic, and social [forces and] changes in a country shaping a new [or evolving] identity? … How can institutions be built so that they absorb the psychological insights and serve as antidote to regressions in the large group and in the interaction of leaders and followers? (Volkan, 1997, p. 206)

Volkan's response to Sadat's speech has been a lifetime of thought and pragmatic strategies for intervention in world conflicts. It may offer all of us a ray of hope that:

> The psychoanalytic study of the psychology of large groups can do much to illuminate this large, shadowy area [of racial, ethnic, religious and political conflict]. Better understanding and application of these ideas may help unveil those irrational and stubborn factors that lead to violence so that they can be dealt with more effectively, so that we can bring our worst enemies—our shared identity conflicts and anxieties—from darkness into light. (Volkan, 1997, p. 227)

Howard B. Levine, M.D.
Faculty, Psychoanalytic Institute of New England East (PINE);
Faculty and Supervising Analyst, Massachusetts Institute
for Psychoanalysis (MIP), Boston, Massachusetts

References

Freud, S. (1915b). Thoughts for the times on war and death. *S. E. 14*: 274–302. London: Hogarth.
Freud, S. (1933b). Why war? *S. E. 22*: 196–215. London: Hogarth.
Volkan, V. D. (1997). *Blood Lines: From Ethnic Pride to Ethnic Terrorism*. New York: Farrar, Straus and Giroux.
Volkan, V. D. (2004). *Blind Trust: Large Groups and Their Leaders in Times of Crisis and Terror*. Charlottesville, VA: Pitchstone.
Volkan, V. D. (2013). *Enemies on the Couch: A Psychopolitical Journey Through War and Peace*. Durham, NC: Pitchstone.

ABOUT THIS BOOK

In 1977, then Egyptian President Anwar el-Sadat stunned the political world by visiting Israel. When he addressed the Israeli Knesset he spoke about a *psychological wall* between Arabs and Israelis, and stated that psychological barriers constitute seventy per cent of all problems existing between the two groups. With the blessings of the Egyptian, Israeli, and American governments, the American Psychiatric Association's Committee on Psychiatry and Foreign Affairs followed up on Sadat's statements by bringing together influential Israelis, Egyptians, and later Palestinians for a series of unofficial negotiations that took place between 1979 and 1986. My membership in this committee, as a psychiatrist and psychoanalyst, initiated my reaching beyond the consulting room into international relations.

Soon after the American Psychiatric Association project ended I founded the Center for the Study of Mind and Human Interaction (CSMHI) under the umbrella of the University of Virginia's School of Medicine in Charlottesville, Virginia. Through my years at CSMHI I headed its interdisciplinary team (including psychoanalysts, psychotherapists, political scientists, former diplomats, and historians) that conducted multi-year unofficial diplomatic dialogues between

Americans and Soviets, Russians and Estonians, Croats and Bosnian Muslims, Georgians and South Ossetians, Turks and Greeks. In addition, we studied post-revolution or post-war societies such as Albania subsequent to dictator Enver Hoxha's rule and Kuwait after the Iraqi invasion. I also worked with traumatised people in refugee camps where individuals were constantly made aware of their large-group identity. In the psychoanalytic literature, the term "large group" often refers to thirty to 150 individuals who meet in order to deal with a given issue. I use the term "large group" to refer to tens, hundreds of thousands, or millions of people, most of whom will never know or see each other, but who share a feeling of sameness—a large-group identity.

I was honoured to be a member of former President Jimmy Carter's International Negotiation Network for nearly two decades, starting in 1980s. I spent some time with other political or religious leaders, such as former Soviet leader Mikhail Gorbachev, the late Yasser Arafat, Estonian president Arnold Rüütel, Turkish president Abdullah Gül and Archbishop Desmond Tutu, and observed aspects of leader–follower psychology up close.

I retired from the University of Virginia in 2002, and in 2008 joined other psychoanalysts (Lord John Alderdice, UK; Edward Shapiro, USA; and Gerard Fromm, USA) and psychoanalytic psychiatrists or group therapists (Abdülkadir Çevik, Turkey; Frank Ochberg, USA; Robi Friedman, Israel; Regine Scholz, Germany; and Coline Covington, UK) in meeting every six months with active or former politicians, political scientists, lawyers, and sociologists from different regions to examine world affairs from a psychopolitical point of view. At the present time this work continues with participants representing Germany, Iran, Israel, Lebanon, Russia, Turkey, United Kingdom, United States, and the West Bank (see: www.internationaldialogueinitiative.com). In short, for over thirty years I have been examining many psychological "walls" in numerous international contexts, and putting my findings into theoretical and practical frames.

When large groups (i.e., tribal, ethnic, national, religious, and political ideological groups) are in conflict, psychological issues contaminate most of their political, economic, legal, or military concerns. People assigned to deal with these conflicts on an official level establish short—and long-term strategies and mobilise resources to implement them. In so doing, they develop assumptions that support psychological advantages for their own group over that of the Other. My focus is on another type of psychology—on human nature in large groups. I will refer to mostly unconscious issues that appear in leader-followers interactions and thwart peaceful, adaptive solutions to large-group conflicts.

In 2013 I published memoirs of my over thirty years of work in international relations, *Enemies on the Couch: A Psychopolitical Journey Through War and Peace* (2013). In it I ask the reader to join me in my journey, observe closely various historical events of the last three decades, meet persons I got to know from different parts of the world, and wonder about shared psychological processes in large groups. It is a book on the history of the world beginning in 1979 as observed from a psychoanalytic angle. After reading that book, some psychoanalytic educators and friends in diplomatic circles urged me to prepare another book that could be used as a direct introduction to psychoanalytic political psychology, with special emphasis on the relationship between psychoanalysis and diplomacy.

This present book, *Psychoanalysis, International Relations, and Diplomacy*, is written for psychoanalysts, other mental health professionals, and those involved in taming international tensions and conflicts. It is based on data most of which were presented in my previously published papers, books, or in lectures I have given internationally over the last decade. Psychoanalytic training does not include politics and international relations. Nevertheless, starting with Sigmund Freud, a number of psychoanalysts have shown interest in large-group human behaviour, political leader–follower relationships, political ideologies, and religion. Especially after the Holocaust, many psychoanalysts began to examine the influence of massive trauma at the hand of the Other and its transgenerational transmission. This volume describes new findings in large-group psychology, and explores collaboration between psychoanalysis and diplomacy. I provide detailed information on historical events and individuals involved in them to illustrate large-group processes and their consequences in a way similar to that of a psychoanalyst presenting the necessary case materials to show the manifestations of a patient's individual psychology. My aim here is to provide a sourcebook on large-group psychology.

Vamık Volkan
Charlottesville, VA

CHAPTER ONE

Diplomats and psychoanalysts

S tarting with Sigmund Freud, psychoanalysts have sought to venture beyond the couch and apply their expertise to inter-connected aspects of human behaviour and the external world. But given the pervasive influence *realpolitik* has had over government and the study of international relations, and some inherent difficul-ties within the field of psychoanalysis, it is not surprising that political science and psychoanalysis still remain distant cousins.

The concept of realpolitik was first introduced by Ludwig von Rochau in his *Grundsätze der Realpolitik* (1853). He advised politicians to estimate carefully what the opposition *really* wanted, not what they *said* they wanted, and to be prepared to exert force when necessary. Eventually the term came to mean the rational evaluation and realistic assessment of the options available to one's large group and one's enemies. In the United States, especially after World War II, this latter interpretation of realpolitik, renamed the "rational actor model," became prevalent in political analysis. This model (in its various forms) assumes that people make decisions by engaging in a rational calculation of costs and benefits, and that leaders, governments, and nations are rational "actors". (For various studies of this model, its modifications, and criticism see Etzioni, 1967; George, 1969; Allison, 1971; Janis & Mann, 1977; Barner-Barry & Rosenwein, 1985; Jervis, Lebow & Stein, 1985; Achen & Snidal, 1989.)

The so-called "deterrence" theories characteristic of the Cold War era depended on this type of rational approach, and many political scholars believe that decisions made according to rational actor models prevented the Soviets and the Americans from using their nuclear arsenals. This is most likely the case, but policies based on deterrence have also failed, and research in a variety of disciplines demonstrated that decisions were not always predictable based on rational assumptions. For example, Egyptian president Anwar el-Sadat surprised both Israeli and the United States military intelligence by launching a massive attack across the Suez Canal on Yom Kippur, 6 October 1973. Based on rational deterrence calculations, policy analysts believed an Egyptian offensive could not be launched before 1975, and so reports on Egyptian troop movements in September 1973 were regarded as merely exercises. As the shortcomings of various rational actor models became evident, some political scientists, and even some government decision-makers and diplomats, began to borrow concepts from cognitive psychology in the late 1970s and early 1980s to explain "faulty" decision making. But they did not look to psychoanalysis for insights.

The application of cognitive psychology nevertheless expanded the scope of analysis of political and international relationships. But the limitations of this approach, which primarily focused on conscious considerations, also became evident. As early as 1977, Janis and Mann, who were considered to be at the forefront of applying cognitive concepts to decision making, were aware of the relevance of unconscious motivations. They suggested a link between disciplines when they noted that, "If the study of unconscious motives that affect decision making is to proceed, it is necessary to take into account other types of research, including psychoanalytic case studies" (p. 98). One of the psychoanalytic cases Janis and Mann studied was Freud's (1905e [1901]) case of Dora, an eighteen-year-old girl whose "decisional conflict," to use the terminology of Janis and Mann, concerned whether or not to have an illicit love affair with Mr K, who was married and a friend of Dora's family. After deciding against the affair, Dora had much post-decisional regret and remained in "post-decisional conflict." Through their review of Freud's findings on the unconscious reasons why Dora could not "work through and resolve the post-decisional conflict in a normal fashion" (Janis & Mann, 1977, p. 100), Janis and Mann noted that psychoanalytic insights were in fact needed to fully understand decision making.

While both cognitive psychology and psychoanalysis consider the influence of previous historical events in decision making, the nature of psychoanalytic theory takes into account more than conscious motivational factors and analogous associations; it examines defensive alterations of early experiences, layered personal meanings of events, condensations of unconscious motivations, transference distortions, and the personality organisation of decision makers. The principle of multiple function and over-determination, first described in detail by Waelder in 1930, has to be considered in the evaluation of each decision-making process as well as diplomatic and political processes.

Although politicians and diplomats began to broaden their horizons in order to understand "faulty" decision making, and political scientists cautiously explored the relevance of psychology, psychoanalysts themselves did not respond quickly to this opportunity to contribute. Instead, it was two diplomats who indirectly invited psychoanalysts to apply their knowledge of internal psychodynamics to international issues. In 1974, following the division of the island of Cyprus, my homeland, into Turkish and Greek sectors, Turkish Prime Minister Bülent Ecevit noted in a public speech the role of psychology in the long-standing conflict between Turkey and Greece. In response to this pertinent observation, I began to study the Cyprus problem, and later with historian Norman Itzkowitz, I studied 1,000 years of Turkish-Greek relations through a psychoanalytic lens (Volkan, 1976; Volkan & Itzkowitz, 1984, 1993–1994).

A few year later, as I have already stated, Egyptian president Anwar el-Sadat indirectly encouraged psychoanalysts to become involved in the study of international relationships. His speech at the Knesset prompted a committee of the American Psychiatric Association (APA) to sponsor a six-year project (1979–1986) that brought together teams of influential Egyptians, Israelis, and Palestinians for a series of unofficial dialogues. The American team, serving as neutral facilitators, consisted of psychoanalysts (including myself), psychiatrists, psychologists, and former diplomats. The Israeli and Arab groups also included psychiatrists and psychoanalysts, but were mostly comprised of influential citizens—ambassadors, a former high-level military officer, journalists, and others—attending the meetings in an unofficial capacity.

Three years later, inspired by my involvement in international and interdisciplinary projects, and encouraged by the writings of Mitscherlich (1971) who urged psychoanalysts to move beyond their clinical offices and become part of interdisciplinary work on societal and political issues, I founded the Center for the Study of Mind and Human Interaction (CSMHI) at the University of Virginia. The faculty of the centre included psychoanalysts, psychiatrists, former diplomats, political scientists, historians, and others from both social and behavioural sciences. We conducted unofficial dialogues with Soviet psychologists and diplomats during the two years prior to the collapse of the Soviet Union, and later worked in locations such as the Baltic Republics, Georgia, Kuwait, Albania, Slovakia, Turkey, Croatia, Germany, the United States, among other places. As far as I know, this centre, which closed three years after my retirement in 2002, was the only organisation that specialised in directly applying psychoanalytic concepts to ethnonational conflicts, post-war adjustments, and facilitation of inter-large-group dialogues to encourage democracy and peaceful coexistence (Volkan, 1988, 1997, 2004, 2006a, 2013).

There were certainly others—our contemporaries and those who preceded us—who made significant contributions to interdisciplinary work and examined history, politics, and social movement and relationships through a psychoanalytic lens. As far back as the 1930s political scientist Harold Lasswell, following trips to Europe and study of psychoanalytic theories, became a voice introducing psychodynamic factors and the role of unconscious issues in political science and politics (Lasswell, 1932, 1936, 1948, 1963). Some psychoanalysts, too, following Freud, also applied psychoanalytic findings to social and political topics including political propaganda (see, for example, Money-Kyrle, 1941; Kris, 1943–1944; Glower, 1947; Fornari, 1966). Notably, in the 1960s with the works of psychoanalysts such as Niederland (1961, 1968) and Krystal (1968), many psychoanalysts began to study the impact of the Holocaust on its survivors and then on the generations to follow. Some of these studies included psychological examination of societal involvement of perpetrators and societal responses to massive trauma (Mitscherlich & Mitscherlich, 1975). References to such papers are too numerous to include here. However, in our book *The Third Reich in the Unconscious* (Volkan, Ast & Greer, 2002) my co-authors and I included many such references (also see: Grubrich-Simitis, 1979; Kogan, 1995; Kestenberg & Brenner, 1996; Laub & Podell, 1997; Brenner, 2001, 2004).

There were other psychoanalysts who made contributions to political and societal issues as well: Moses (1982) examined the Arab-Israeli conflict from a psychoanalytic point of view. Šebek (1992, 1994) studied societal responses to living under communism in Europe. Loewenberg (1995) went back to the history of the Weimar Republic and emphasised its humiliation and economic collapse as major factors in creating shared personality characteristics among the German youth and their embrace of Nazi ideology. Kakar (1996) described the effects of Hindu-Muslim religious conflict in Hyderabad, India. Apprey (1993, 1998) focused on the influence of transgenerational transmission of trauma on African Americans and their culture, while Adams (1996) warned us not to ignore race and colour in psychoanalysis. Hollander (1997) explored events in South America. In addition, Afaf Mahfouz from Bethesda, Maryland and Vivian Pender from New York, New York played key roles in promoting links between psychoanalysts and the UN. Similarly, in 1998 South American psychoanalysts organised a large and success-ful meeting in Lima, Peru that brought psychoanalysts together with high-level diplomats and politicians. The list goes on.

After 11 September 2001 psychoanalysts were highly motivated to study trauma at the hand of the Other. The International Psychoana-lytic Association (IPA) formed the Terror and Terrorism Study Group chaired by Norwegian analyst Sverre Varvin that lasted for several years (Varvin & Volkan, 2003) and established a committee in the United Nations. The theme of the 44th Annual Meeting of the IPA in Rio de Janeiro in the summer of 2005 was "trauma", including trauma due to historical events. Hollander (2010) examined psychopolitical aspects of the United States after 11 September 2001. Meanwhile, Elliott, Bishop and Stokes (2004) and Lord Alderdice (2007, 2010) wrote about the situation in Northern Ireland, and Roland (2011) described in great detail the continuing influence the India-Pakistan partition had on the populations there. Erlich (2010, 2013) examined the concept of enemy, wounded societies, prejudice and paranoia in large groups, and the ter-rorist mind. Böhm and Kaplan (2011) explored the concept of revenge, and Fromm (2012) reviewed transgenerational transmissions. In 2011 during her plenary lecture at the American Psychoanalytic Associa-tion's Winter Meeting in New York, outgoing president Prudence Gourguechon urged the members of the association to show their faces in areas already in the public eye. She stated that if psychoanalysts do not explain the causality of disturbing events and provide professional information about human behaviour, statements by others with less knowledge on such matters will prevail.

Nevertheless, collaboration between psychoanalysis and politics or diplomacy remained, and still remains, limited. It has proven difficult to define specific areas where cooperation between these disciplines can occur in useful and mutually satisfying ways. One reason stems from psychoanalytic traditions and previous attempts to apply psychoanalysis to other areas. Starting with Sigmund Freud, psychoanalysts have written on a variety of topics relating to the diplomatic and political realms, but their contributions have thus far been mostly theoretical in nature, and of little practical use to diplomats and politicians. Psychoanalysts have studied group psychology, political leaders, and their relationships with followers, political propaganda, mass violence and war. They have developed theories on the aggressive drive as the root cause of war, the perception of a state or nation as a mother, groups who respond to a leader as to a father, and identification of group members with one another. Frequently and unfortunately, they applied psychodynamic observations of small groups, such as therapy groups composed of six to twelve individuals or organisations with members in the hundreds, to the psychodynamics of large groups composed of tens, hundreds of thousands, or millions of individuals. Few theorists accounted for differences between the processes that occur in a stable large group and those that occur when a large group is regressed, or whether or not a large group is preoccupied with a neighbouring group.

Freud's (1921c) theory on group psychology, which reflects an oedipal theme, is well known. But we also must remember that Freud, as Waelder (1971) stated, was *only* speaking of regressed groups, and his theory does not provide a full explanation of large-group psychology. Nevertheless, Freud's theory of group psychology should not be fully abandoned. The behaviour he described can be seen in regressed groups today: the members of the group sublimate their aggression against the leader in a way that is similar to the process of a son turning his negative feelings towards his oedipal father into loyalty. In turn, the members of a group idealise the leader, identify with each other, and rally around the leader.

Some international events illustrate Freud's ideas in concrete fashion. In 1998 tension between the US and Iraq increased over the issue of inspection of some of Saddam Hussein's numerous presidential "palaces" in which illegal weapons were reportedly being manufactured. Some Iraqis responded to the increased tension and possible US military action by creating a "human shield" around his palaces and other important sites. These individuals were *literally* rallying around a leader. Although autocratic persuasion and propaganda certainly played a role in their response, many reputable policy analysts believed that a majority of these Iraqis acted voluntarily. In 2013 we also see literal rallying around a leader in isolated and regressed North Korea.

Given shortcomings in Freud's ideas on group psychology, in the 1970s and 1980s some psychoanalysts have shifted their approach on large groups from emphasising the leader as an idealised father, to the mental representation of a large group as an idealised and nurturing mother. For example, Anzieu (1971, 1984), Chasseguet-Smirgel (1984), and Kernberg (1980, 1989) wrote on regressed groups and its members' shared fantasies in which the large group represents an idealised, all-gratifying early mother ("breast-mother") that repairs all narcissistic lesions. The members of such regressed large groups, according to Anzieu and Chasseguet-Smirgel, will choose leaders who promote such illusions of gratification, and the large group may become violent and try to destroy external reality that it perceives as interfering with this illusion. Thus, there seemed to be among some psychoanalysts a growing emphasis on pre-oedipal rather than oedipal issues on this subject. Kernberg stated that Freud's description of libidinal ties among the members of a group in fact reflects a defence against pre-oedipal conditions.

The above formulations basically represent individuals' perceptions of large groups and political leaders, and therefore remain theoretical constructs that political scientists or diplomats find difficult to use in their own examination of day-to-day events or important international incidents. These formulations do not reflect a *large-group psychology in its own right*. What does this mean? There are echoes of individual psychology in large-group psychology shared by tens, hundreds of thousands, or millions of persons, but we recognise that a large group is not the same as a single, standalone person. Yet multitudes of people in a large group do share a psychological journey, such as complicated mourning after major shared losses at the hand of the Other, or when they use the same psychological mechanism such as "externalisation" of unwanted images that makes the Other a shared target. These journeys become sustained social, cultural, political, or ideological processes that are *specific* for the large group under study. Considering large-group psychology in its own right means making formulations as to a large group's conscious and unconscious shared psychological experiences and motivations that initiate specific social, cultural, political, or ideological processes, processes that influence this large group's internal and external affairs. We recognise this same process of evaluation in psychoanalysts' clinical practices when they make formulations about the internal worlds of their patients in order to summarise diagnoses and treatments.

In large-group psychology I noted that shared social, cultural, political, or ideological processes are primarily in the service of protecting the narcissistic investment in what is commonly known as the large-group identity, such as an ethnic or religious identity, and its integrity. Leader–follower interactions comprise only one element of this effort. Wars, war-like situations, terrorism, diplomatic efforts, and shared losses and gains associated with shared mourning or elation are all carried out in the name of large-group identity, an *abstract* concept. This is true even though this psychological source is usually hidden behind rational real-world considerations—economic, legal, or political.

We observe various types of narcissistic investment in large-group identity. A healthy degree of narcissistic investment in a large-group identity provides a sense of belonging and trans-generational continuity among members, and in turn supports their individualised self-esteem. An "exaggerated large-group narcissism" denotes a process in which people in a given large group become preoccupied with the superiority of almost anything connected with their large-group identity, ranging from nursery rhymes and food, to established cultural customs, artistic achievements, scientific discoveries, past historical triumphs, and possession of more powerful weapons than their neighbours, even when such perceptions and beliefs may not be realistic. A particularly pernicious form of "malignant large-group narcissism" is observable when members of one large group share a spoken or unspoken belief that "inferior others" are contaminating their group's superiority, and they feel entitled to use shared sadism in order to oppress or kill them. What happened in Nazi Germany illustrates this concept. There are even large groups that exhibit "masochistic large-group narcissism". For example, the members may hold on to a sense of victimisation for decades or even centuries after a massive trauma at the hand of the Other, often in the service of feeling morally superior, openly or in a hidden fashion.

My efforts to develop a large-group psychology in its own right and to study the crucial role of large-group identity in this psychology began with my participation in small meetings in which Israeli and Arab representatives were brought together. I noted that besides speaking about their own individual identities, expectations and anxieties, and besides the evidence of small-group dynamics such as those described by Bion (1961), participants from antagonistic groups became spokespersons for the large groups to which they belonged. All participants in the dialogue, regardless of their personality organisation, professional or social standing, or political orientation, felt that their side was under personal attack and were compelled to defend the narcissism invested in their large group. Since individuals seemed determined to protect their large group's identity, I came to believe that large-group identity needed to be studied more fully. I concluded that understanding how a large group's identity develops, how it has to be protected, especially under stress, how large groups will tolerate sadism or masochism, or feel entitled to make others suffer or even suffer themselves in order to maintain their large-group identity, are crucial issues of large-group psychology in its own right. In the next chapter I will examine large-group identity in depth. Now, we will return to Freud's times.

Writing in 1932, in a letter to Albert Einstein, Freud (1933b) was pessimistic about human nature and the role of psychoanalysis in stopping wars or war-like situations. Although Arlow (1973) also found some cautious optimism in Freud's later writings on this subject, Freud's pessimism was mirrored by many of his followers, and this may also have played a role historically in the limited contributions made to diplomacy by psychoanalysts. Having seen what human beings are capable of doing to their fellow humans in many parts of the world over the last three decades, I cannot help but join Freud in his pessimism. Large groups of people cannot completely refrain from committing acts of violence, mass destruction, and atrocities. Thus, it is better for us, as psychoanalysts or psychotherapists, to consider a more practical approach to international relationships. In certain cases we may be able to contribute to the prevention of mass aggressive expressions. We may be able to offer insights that help large groups and their leaders cope with traumatic events so that enmity between large groups will not end up repeating endless cycles of violence. And perhaps we can encourage greater understanding about decision making and more flexibility when political attitudes and policies become narrow and rigid.

But on the subject of how we can contribute to and influence international relationships, there is one more aspect of Freud's legacy that we must consider. Erlich (2013) clearly illustrates Freud's struggle in integrating his Jewish identity with other identities in Vienna. It seems evident that he had assimilated, possibly without being aware of it, a degree of European ethnocentrism and a tendency to stereotype and denigrate other cultures. In his correspondence with Einstein, Freud made certain racist remarks about "Turks and Mongols", and also jokingly referred to his patients as Negroes (Tate, 1996). These were not necessarily vicious or hateful attacks, and racism in general was especially prevalent and to a degree accepted in late nineteenth— and early twentieth-century Europe. Freud may have identified with the aggressor in an attempt to defend against mounting anti-Semitism. But his remarks nevertheless serve to remind us that our own personal analysis, self-analysis, and our extensive study of and training in human nature do not easily free us from investment in certain cultural norms, the attitudes of our own large group, or even racism. To be most effective in the psychoanalytic examination of large-group processes, and to appropriately apply certain psychoanalytic insights to international or interethnic issues, psychoanalytic candidates must study large-group psychology in its own right at psychoanalytic institutes. And when the opportunity presents itself, psychoanalysts should become involved in interdisciplinary work, gain first-hand experience with many cultures, and work through their own prejudices as much as possible. Furthermore, I long ago concluded that, just as I would not professionally treat a family member or a friend, I would not conduct an unofficial diplomatic project in which my own original large group was a party.

So far I have summarised some of the theoretical considerations and traditions from the times of Freud that have prevented psychoanalysts from significantly contributing to the understanding of human large-group relationships beyond the couch. But other differences between the disciplines of psychoanalysis and diplomacy present difficulties that also should be mentioned.

The nature of the two fields, as they are typically practised, creates obstacles that prevent psychoanalysts and diplomats from working together. In clinical work, a psychoanalyst or psychotherapist becomes involved in a long process that aims to help the patient resolve conflicts, be more realistic about everyday life, and become more flexible and playful without experiencing excessive anxiety, depression, or guilt. The aim of the psychoanalyst is to find the best possible solution for the patient's problems. Psychoanalysts or psychotherapists typically need to make money through their profession, and hopefully receive personal satisfaction from helping others, but otherwise are not primarily driven by self-interest.

Much diplomacy, on the other hand, with the possible exception of those aspects that seek only to encourage cross-cultural understanding, concerns defining the "national interest" or another type of large-group interest in a given situation, and bargaining to protect or extend this interest. Although others may benefit from policies implemented through diplomacy, it is in essence self-serving. In some cases, it may be in the national or another type of large-group interest to encourage, maintain, or ignore a conflict rather than seek its resolution.

Some psychoanalysts who have worked with diplomats have been appalled when diplomats demand short, simple, and quick advice or solutions. Such an approach goes against psychoanalysts' training and thinking, since in clinical practice they focus on multiple internal and external motivations and their intertwining, and favour an open-ended process. On the other hand, most psychoanalysts do not put themselves in diplomats' shoes and have no experiential knowledge of diplomatic training, practices, and traditions. Furthermore, going through psychoanalytic training does not prepare psychoanalysts to act as consultants in diplomatic efforts. They need to gain in-depth knowledge of the issues at hand, the history of the groups involved, and the ability to tolerate and enjoy interdisciplinary cooperation.

There are accepted rituals when the diplomats of opposing groups come together. Diplomacy is mainly based on obsessional patterns that try to keep anxiety from interfering with intellectualised considerations. Inevitable prejudice and transference distortions are always absorbed in this obsessional process, especially when a diplomat's large group is under stress, threat, or is regressed. In effect, under stressful conditions, at official negotiations every component of large-group identity is enhanced and dominates motivations. This leads to even more ritualisations in which "playfulness" and the search for creative solutions often dissolve into resistances to the slow process of change. And even those diplomats who might want to negotiate creatively, or have "orders" from their governments to try to reach agreements, may adopt rigidified ritualisations. Diplomats' patterns and aims need to be clearly understood by psychoanalysts if collaboration between them is ever to be fruitful.

Such problematic dynamics are further compounded by other motivations. Vasquez (1986) wrote that "the most persistent philosophical question" to plague official diplomats has been "whether the foreign policy of a state ought to be based on the norms and principles of moral conduct" (p. 1). Official diplomacy speaks of *Fiat justitia, pereat mundus* (Let justice be done, though the world perish) and seeks to galvanise its constituency by invoking images of glory and honor as they devalue the opposing large group or take up arms against a foe. Ethnic, nationalistic, religious, economic, and social issues are often used to fuel such "truthfulness" of one's position and "immoral" aspects of the opposition's views and activities. The Christian Crusades and the Muslim holy wars were each pitched as a high purpose in which the Almighty was a partner. When the US invaded Panama in 1989, resulting in the capture of a drug lord at the expense of countless innocent victims, the incursion was called "Operation Just Cause" echoing Thomas Aquinas. The precise definition of morality can become not only ambiguous, but also corrupted when threatened by the losses of power, self-esteem, and self-determination that are often connected with large-group identity issues.

Brenner (1983) believed that morality, formed at the oedipal age, begins as a matter of feeling, thinking, and behaving in ways to avoid punishment. Children's oedipal conflicts bring fears of losing loved ones and/or their love, and of being punished. Children then become "moral" in the way their fantasies dictate in order to minimise anxiety and depressive feelings. They may identify with their perceptions of a forbidding parent or remove themselves from competition in an effort to avoid expected punishment. And, since the beginning of morality is linked to anxiety or depressive feelings, the more anxiety and depressive feelings the child has, the stricter the superego he or she may develop: the outcome is a compelling sense of morality that is equal to the compelling need to avoid punishment. As children grow, they develop more sophisticated anxiety-reducing mechanisms and moral codes that are unrelated to the fear of punishment. Moreover, they take into account the moral code of whatever group, large or small, they come to owe allegiance to and, reciprocally, the group's code either corresponds to their psychological needs or is rejected. With this premise in mind, one is not surprised to find that moral sense is not to be relied upon in situations in which there are regressive tendencies.

At times of stress, nations, ethnic communities, or other large groups may undergo mass regression in which collectively experienced unconscious anxiety becomes condensed with a fear of the Other. Consequently, the compromise formations upon which the large group's shared moral code is based are disturbed, and new "moralities" evolve in dealing with antagonists who are usually, at this point, stereotypes. In 1942, the US government's "morality" allowed the internment of Japanese Americans because, according to Loewenberg (1995), there was a mass regression in the United States. The government's decision was irrational and illegal. "It was not founded in reality because there was not a single demonstrated case of espionage by a Japanese American. It was irrational because the relatively large Japanese Nisei and Sansei populations of the exposed Hawaiian Islands were not interned" (Loewenberg, 1995, p. 167).

When large groups in conflict are regressed, their official negotiators are more prone to hold on to the components of their large-group identity, to utilise more externalisations of unwanted internalised self—or object images and projections of unacceptable thoughts and affects, and to protect themselves more stubbornly from the return of their externalisations and projections (*boomerang effect*). These defence mechanisms lead to less empathy for the opposing large group's problems and create resistances to attitude changes and willingness to compromise. The "therapeutic regression" or "regression in the service of the ego" (Kris, 1952) that is part of our clinical vocabulary and necessary for a successful clinical outcome is rarely found in official diplomatic negotiations.

A therapeutic regression of an individual on a psychoanalyst's couch refers to taming a patient's existing and chaotic regression and replacing it with circumscribed, controlled, and reversible regression; these become initial steps of progression. There is no parallel concept or technique in official diplomatic interactions for evolving such a process of change. Typically, opposing sides reach agreement, but not through a therapeutic regression followed by progression. Instead it happens through the utilisation of denial, dissociation, and repression of aspects of the existing conflicts, isolating from emotions pertaining to conflict, and rationalising the acceptance of terms of negotiation. If the parties in conflict ask the help of a third, "neutral" team from another country, the third party representatives may interfere with the malignant effects of the existing chaotic regression among the representatives of opposing groups. Transference distortions often occur in official diplomatic inter- actions between the members of opposing large groups, but, although psychoanalysts are trained to deal with them, diplomats typically accept such distortions by utilising rationalisations.

When agreements are reached and signed by opposing large groups, the conflicts and emotions exacerbated by regression during crises do not altogether disappear and are not fully tamed, but are pushed into the shadows. These conflicts and emotions may erupt later to create new crises. The rule of law and reality testing, such as a lack of resources to remain at war, force parties in conflict to adjust slowly to terms of agree- ments and remain at peace. Nevertheless, legal documents do not sub- stantially change enemy relationships as far as internal perceptions and mental experiences are concerned. War-like situations and even wars themselves, therefore can remain an imminent but repressed threat. However, diplomatically negotiated terms of peace are not necessarily always doomed. New events, such as a friendship between the lead- ers of enemy large groups, internal change, or a revolution within one large group, can lead to the modification of perceptions, emotions, and expectations of the Other at a psychological level.

These are a few examples of how various phenomena appear in the daily work of both psychoanalysts and diplomats, but are perceived and reacted to differently. In spite of such inherent difficulties, there is nevertheless still room for cooperation. Sometimes, when diplomats facilitate negotiations between enemy large groups, they become frus- trated when minor differences (Freud, 1918a, 1930a) become significant obstacles in negotiations; psychoanalysts may help to design strategies that allow individual identities and large-group identities to be main- tained and avoid the anxiety that can be experienced when too much "sameness" is perceived by opposing groups. Psychoanalysis also can advise diplomacy about the importance of psychological borders— "togetherness" between ethnic groups, for example, can work better when some form of psychological border between the opponents is maintained. Psychoanalysts can be consultants when transference and countertransference reactions between opposing parties become sticky.

In areas where there are chronic conflicts between two large groups, third-party facilitators may become frustrated because leaders or dip- lomats of opposing large groups keep talking about past events instead of focusing on current issues. When conducting an official dialogue, facilitators typically want the representatives of the groups in conflict to focus on real issues and make progress towards concrete objectives, but the representatives often insist on enumerating in detail their group's historical grievances. (Later in this book I refer to them as "chosen traumas".) A psychoanalytic perspective can be useful in such situations since psychoanalysts' training and practice have taught them that no progress will be made on present issues if past ones are not understood and explored. A psychoanalyst can therefore help those in the dialogue understand the necessity of discussing chosen traumas and help to expand time when past and present have collapsed. Most importantly, psychoanalysts can team up with former diplomats, historians, and others for certain suitable projects that are often called "unofficial diplomacy" or "track two diplomacy" (Davidson & Montville, 1981–1982).

At the present time wide-spread terrorism, modern globalisation, much increased voluntary and forced migrations, incredible advances in technology, and related factors are forcing humans to face and experience a new type of civilisation that includes recognition of the fact that old-type diplomacy under the influence of *realpolitik* is no longer effective in many areas of international relations and conflicts. In the attempts to stabilise, maintain, or repair large-group identities, we still see shared hostile or malignant prejudices and other psychological obstacles getting in the way of a peaceful world. Therefore, further understanding of large-group psychology in its own right has become a necessity.

CHAPTER TWO

Large-group identity, shared prejudice, chosen glories, and chosen traumas

B elonging to a large group is a natural phenomenon of human life. Large groups are known as tribes; clans; ethnic, nationalistic, racial or religious entities; or believers in and followers of a political ideology since childhood. Membership in a large group is an antidote to loneliness; it provides self-esteem on an individual level and on many occasions gives people pleasure and lifts their spirits. This chapter, however, is on one of its least desirable by-products: shared prejudice against the members of another large group.

Shared prejudice can be benign, hostile, or malignant, and is known in the political science, history, and related literature by various names. When the underlying shared prejudice is revealed, then making distinctions among us-and-them terms, such as *racism, neo-racism, apartheid, ethnocentrism, ethnic hatred, fascism, anti-Semitism, Islamophobia, anti-Westernisation, anti-guest workers, xenophobia, national or religious exceptionalism*, focuses only on differences between various historical events and reasons for their longevity. Such distinctions are necessary in order to clarify situations as they exist today. For example, traditional racism is discrimination based on a pseudo-scientific thesis that there is a specific inequality between races that is reflected in the "deficient" personality, intellect, and culture of members of the "lower" races. Neo-racism stresses a wider, more anthropological basis, such as family structure, social value systems, language, and religion, as justification to keep large groups separate.

To understand prejudice shared by tens, hundreds of thousands, or millions of individuals we first need to explore what *large-group identity* is. Large-group identities are articulated in terms of commonality such as, "We are Apache," "We are Basque," "We are Catholics," "We are capitalist," and/or "You are Orthodox Jews," "You are Arab," "You are Muslim," "You are communist."

Now, I will describe how an individual's identity develops and becomes linked to his or her large-group identity, and then explore how the shared large-group identity and shared prejudice become intertwined.

Freud and early psychoanalysts seldom referred to the term "identity". It was Erikson (1956, 1959) who made it a psychoanalytic one and described it as a subjective experience of a persistent sense of sameness within oneself. In everyday life, an adult individual typically refers to his or her social or professional status. A person may simultaneously perceive him—or herself as mother or father, physician or carpenter, or someone who enjoys specific sports or recreational activities. These facets fit the definition of identity on the surface but do not fully reflect a person's sense of emotional and bodily continuity in the self experience: the past, present, and future are integrated into a smooth continuum of remembered, felt, and expected existence for the individual (Akhtar, 1999). There is also a strong link between one's personal identity and one's large-group identity from childhood on.

"Identity" needs to be differentiated from related concepts such as an individual's "character" and "personality," which are usually used interchangeably. The latter terms describe others' impressions of the individual's emotional expressions, modes of speech, typical actions, and habitual ways of thinking and behaving. If we observe someone to be habitually clean, orderly, or greedy, or if he uses excessive intellectualisation, shows excessive ambivalence and controlled emotional expressions, we say that this person has an obsessional character. If we observe someone who is overtly suspicious and cautious, and whose physical demeanor suggests that he or she is constantly scanning the environment for possible danger, we say that this person has a paranoid personality. Unlike the terms "character" and "personality", "identity" refers to an individual's inner working model—he or she, not an outsider, senses and experiences it.

Scientific observations of infants in the last few decades have revealed that an infant's mind is more active than we thought it was. The interplay between age-appropriate experiences and the maturation of the central nervous system in the development of what psychoanalysts call "ego functions" and ability to form mental images of relationships with others ("object relations") have been scientifically studied, especially since the 1970s (see for example, Stern, 1985; Emde, 1991; Lehtonen, 2003; Bloom, 2010). Nevertheless, some observable psychological journeys that infants and small children go through remain the same. One crucial task for small children is coming to see themselves as psychologically separate from their caretakers. As their minds develop, they psychologically push mothers and other caregivers away in order, as Mahler would say, to "separate and individuate" (Mahler & Furer, 1968). Stern (1985) reminds us that an infant is fed four to six times a day, and each feeding experience produces different degrees of pleasure. As the infant grows up, in a sense, different experiences become categorised in the child's mind as "good" and "bad". Loving and frustrating, as well as loved and frustrated, aspects of people connected with these experiences too are divided until the integrative function is effectively accomplished. Small children learn and feel that the mother (or other caretaker) who gratifies them and the mother who frustrates them is the same person, and, correspondingly, the loved and rejected child is also a single individual. The child's *subjective sense* of self, differentiated from the other and integrated, is the child's core personal identity. If the child cannot fully accomplish differentiation and integration, due to biological as well as environmental reasons, the individual's identity, also in adulthood, remains weak, divided, even fragmented.

An infant and a very small child is, to use Erikson's (1966) term, a *generalist* as far as tribal affiliation, nationality, ethnicity, religion, or political ideology are concerned. Kris (1975) also stated that to keep large groups apart is not inborn in human nature. But, there is a psychobiological potential for *we-ness*, and bias toward our own kind (Emde, 1991). Bloom (2010) reminds us that a three-month-old baby is attracted to the face of a person from the same race and young children like to wear the same colour or style shirt as adults in their group. However, because the environment of an infant and very small child is restricted to parents, siblings, relatives, and other caregivers, the extent of "we-ness" does not include a distinct intellectual dimension of ethnicity, nationality, or other type of large-group identity. Therefore, Erikson's and Kris' statements remain correct.

The concept of *identification* is well-known for its role in how children develop not only their personal identity, but also their large-group identity. Children identify with realistic, fantasised, wished-for, or scary aspects of important individuals in their environment. This includes these individuals' mothering, fathering, sibling, and mentoring functions and psychological ways of handling problems. Children also identify with investments in concrete or abstract identity markers or, as Kris (1975) called them, "common symbols of identification" (p. 468). These markers, such as physical body characteristics, language, nursery rhymes, food, dances, religious beliefs, myths, flags, geographical investments, heroes, martyrs, and images of historical events are taken in by children as belonging to them and utilised to expand their internal worlds in relating to their own small groups, and when they get older to their large groups as well. The subjective experience and deep intellectual knowledge of belonging to a large-group identity becomes crystallised later in childhood. Such sharing of sentiments applies as well to those who are members of a politically ideological group, to whose ideology their parents and the important people in their childhood environment subscribed. To become a follower of a political ideology as an adult encompasses other psychological motivations.

Existing conditions in the environment direct children to invest in various types of large-group belongingness. A child born in Hyderabad, India, for example, would focus on religious/cultural issues while developing a large-group identity, since adults there define their dominant large-group identity according to Muslim or Hindu religious affiliation (Kakar, 1996). Questions of investment in ethnicity versus religion, or nationality versus race, or one ideology versus another are not as essential to understanding the psychodynamic processes of linking individual identity to large-group identity and how large groups use them in their interactions. Some children have parents who belong to two different ethnic or religious groups. If an international conflict erupts between these two large groups, these youngsters may, even as adults, have severe psychological problems. In the Republic of Georgia after the collapse of the Soviet Union, wars between Georgians and South Ossetians especially confused and psychologically disturbed individuals with "mixed" lineage. The same was true in Transylvania for the children born of mixed Romanian and Hungarian marriages when the hostility between these two large groups was inflamed (Volkan, 2006a, 2013).

During the adolescent passage there is a psychobiological review that we carry within ourselves. Youngsters loosen their investments in the images of important others of their childhood, modifying, sometimes strengthening, and even disregarding their identifications with them. Furthermore, they add additional identifications, this time through their experiences with their peer group, or far beyond their restricted family or neighbourhood environment (Blos, 1979). Through these internal activities there is an overhauling of youngsters' persistent sense of inner sameness. The formation of a solid individual identity finalises during this period along with large-group identity. Belonging to a large group, after going through the adolescence passage, endures throughout a lifetime (Volkan, 1988, 1997, 2013). A large group's investment in certain symbols or identity markers can be modified after revolutions, wars, or the rule of charismatic leaders. When this happens, the members of the large group also change their investments in these symbols or identity markers. For example, after the Ottoman Empire collapsed and a new Turkey was born, men there stopped wearing the fez and started wearing Western-style hats.

Sometimes an individual's belongingness can be hidden, as we sometimes see in persons after voluntary or forced migrations, in individuals who become dissenters, or in persons who, for ideological and politically influenced reasons, intellectually refuse to belong to any given large group. It is my observation, however, that after the adolescence passage people cannot change the narcissistic investment in their core large-group identity, only hide it. Only rarely through some long-lasting drastic and complicated historical events may a group of individuals evolve a new and very different large-group identity. One example of this was when certain southern Slavs became Bosnian Muslims while under the rule of the Ottoman Empire, which lasted for centuries (Itzkowitz, 1972; Pinson, 1994).

There are two other concepts that closely relate to identification and are utilised in connecting individual identity with large-group identity and helping a child move from being a *generalist* to becoming a member of a large group. I call the first concept "depositing". In identification, children are the primary active actors in collecting images and tasks from their environment and making these images and tasks their own. In depositing, it is the adult in the child's environment who has a psychological urgency to put something—an image associated with certain psychological tasks—into the developing child's psyche. This process fits well into Klein's (1946) description of "projective identification." However, since I am describing the creation of a kind of "psychological DNA" within the child—a foundation for identity formation— I prefer to use the term "depositing", thereby differentiating this term from projective identification in everyday use. Kestenberg's (1982) term "transposition" and Faimberg's (2005) description of "the telescoping of generations" refer to depositing traumatised images; however, these authors do not describe clearly how this process takes place.

In order to understand what "depositing" is, I will now turn my attention to the so-called *replacement child phenomenon* (see, for example: Cain & Cain, 1964; Ainslie & Solyom, 1986; Volkan & Ast, 1997). A mother's first child dies, and when she delivers a second child, she treats the new child, mostly without being aware of it, as if the new child also represents the first. Sometimes the replacement child is given the name of the dead child, is put in the crib or bed of the dead child, and is asked to play with the dead child's toys and smile like the dead child used to smile. The new child has no experiences with the dead one; it is the mother (or a mothering person) who gives tasks to the new child to keep the dead child "alive". Replacement children, due to many genetic and environmental factors, adjust to this psychological situation in many different ways.

Adults who are severely traumatised may also deposit their traumatised self-images into the developing identities of their children. In the clinical setting I studied closely the life of a man who, as a child, was a "reservoir" of the extremely traumatised image of his father-figure who had been a survivor of the 1941 Bataan Death March and the Japanese prison camps in the Philippines. This man grew up and became a sadistic animal killer because the task that was deposited in him was to be a "hunter", instead of being a hunted one as his father-figure had been (Volkan, 2014). Within the psychoanalytic literature there are many examples of how some survivors of the Holocaust have passed images and tasks to their offspring, and how the offspring have psychologically responded to such transgenerational transmissions in ways ranging from being creative to being troublesome (see, for example: Laub & Auerhahn, 1993; Kogan, 1995; Volkan, Ast & Greer, 2002; Brenner, 1999, 2004). Through being reservoirs of deposited images and tasks given to them to deal with these images, children's psychology becomes linked to the history of their families and these families' large-group histories, especially their traumatic elements.

"Depositing" *in large-group psychology* refers to a process shared by tens, hundreds of thousands, or millions that starts in childhood and becomes like a shared "psychological DNA", creating a sense of belonging. After experiencing a collective catastrophe inflicted by an enemy group, affected individuals are left with self-images similarly (though not identically) traumatised by the massive event. They will face difficult tasks taming and rendering harmless the following psychological features:

1. A sense of victimisation and feeling dehumanised.
2. A sense of humiliation due to being helpless.
3. A sense of survival guilt: staying alive while family members, friends, and others die.
4. Difficulty being assertive without facing humiliation.
5. An increase in externalisations/projections.
6. Exaggeration of "bad" prejudice.
7. Hunger for libidinal objects and a search to internalise them.
8. An increase in narcissistic investment in large-group identity.
9. Envy towards the victimiser and (defensive) identification with the oppressor.
10. A sense of unending mourning due to significant losses.

Tens, hundreds of thousands, or millions of individuals deposit traumatised images due to the same event into their children and give them tasks such as: "Regain my self-esteem for me," "Put my mourning process on the right track," "Be assertive and take revenge," or "Never forget and remain alert." It is this transgenerational conveyance of long-term "tasks" that perpetuates the cycle of societal trauma at the hand of the Other.

Though each child in the second generation has his or her own individualised identity, all share similar links to the same massive trauma's image, its mental double, and similar unconscious tasks for coping with it. If the next generation cannot effectively fulfill their shared tasks— and this is usually the case—they will pass these tasks on to the third generation, and so on. Such conditions create a powerful unseen network among a countless number of people. Similar processes may also appear in the descendants of victimisers. Among the descendants of perpetrators there is more preoccupation with consequences of shared feelings of *guilt* than preoccupation with the shared feeling of helplessness. Both groups share a severe difficulty or inability to mourn (Mitscherlich & Mitscherlich, 1975; Volkan, 1997, 2006a, 2013).

As decades pass, the mental image of the ancestors' historical event, with references to heroes and martyrs, continues to link all the individuals in the large group. For the new generations, the meaning of the above tasks goes through what psychoanalysts call *change of function* (Waelder, 1930); now the mental image of the event is used to link all members of the large group together. When an ancestors' massive trauma takes this course I call the shared mental image of the ancestors' trauma a *chosen trauma*—chosen to become a most significant large-group identity marker (Volkan, 1988, 1997, 2004, 2006a, 2013).

Not all past massive tragedies at the hands of the Other evolve as chosen traumas. We see the mythologising of victimised heroes; we hear moving stories associated with a trauma popularised in songs and poetry; and we see political leaders of later times create a preoccupation with a past trauma and related events, turning this historic event into a chosen trauma. In April 2010, Polish President Lech Kaczyński, his wife Maria Kaczyńska, and many of Poland's highest military and civilian leaders were killed in an airplane crash on their way to a ceremony during the anniversary of the Katyn Forest massacre of Polish nationals by Russians that occurred in April–May 1940. I believe that this plane crash will play a role in turning the Katyn massacre into a chosen trauma.

Chosen traumas are specific for each large group. For example, Russians recall the centuries-old "memory" of the Tatar invasion; Serbians hold on to the image of the 1389 Battle of Kosovo; Greeks link themselves when they share the "memory" of the fall of Constantinople (Istanbul) to the Turks in 1453; Czechs commemorate the 1620 Battle of Bilá Hora, which led to their subjugation under the Hapsburg Empire for nearly 300 years; Turks share the "memory" of the defeat of Ottomans on 12 September 1683 at the gates of Vienna; Scots keep alive the story of the Battle of Culloden of 1746 when Bonnie Prince Charlie failed to restore a Stuart to the British throne; the Dakota people of the United States recall the anniversary of their decimation at Wounded Knee in 1890; and Crimean Tatars define themselves by the collective suffering of their deportation from Crimea in 1944. Jews around the globe, including those not personally affected by the Holocaust, all, to some degree, define their large-group identity by direct or indirect reference to the Holocaust. The Holocaust is still too "hot" to be considered a truly established chosen trauma, but it has already become an ethnic marker, even though Orthodox Jews still refer to the 586 BC destruction of the Jewish temple in Jerusalem by Nebuchadnezzar II of Babylonia as the chosen trauma of the Jews. Some chosen traumas are difficult to detect because they are not simply connected to one well recognised historical event. For example, the Estonians' chosen trauma is the fact that they lived under almost constant dominance (Swedes, Germans, and Russians) for thousands of years.

When individuals regress, they "go back" and repeat their childhood experiences contaminated with unconscious fantasies, mental defences, and childhood ways of dealing with conflicts. The things they repeat are specific to them. When a large group regresses, it also "goes back", reactivates, and inflames chosen traumas as well as chosen glories. Chosen glories refer to shared mental representations of a historical event and heroic persons attached to it that are heavily mythologised over time. Chosen glories are passed on to succeeding generations through trans-generational transmissions made in parent/teacher-child interactions and through participation in ritualistic ceremonies recalling past successful events. Chosen glories link children of a large group with each other and with their large group, and the children experience increased self-esteem by being associated with such glories.

While no complicated psychological processes are involved when chosen glories are reactivated, the reactivation of chosen traumas, in supporting large-group identity and its cohesiveness, is more complex. Chosen traumas are more complicated, and stronger, large-group amplifiers. Often chosen glories and chosen traumas are intertwined.

The second concept utilised in connecting individual identity with large-group identity I call *suitable targets of externalisation*. I can explain this concept by expanding the idea that is known in psychoanalysis as *stranger anxiety*: infants' recognition that not all the faces around them belong to their caregivers (Spitz, 1965). A normal phenomenon in human development, stranger anxiety creates the Other in the infant's mind and becomes the source for future "normal" prejudice. When infants become children they also begin to notice that not everything in their environment belongs to their large group. Adults in children's environment provide them with what I call *shared targets*, mostly inanimate things, the utilisation of which "teaches" children *experientially* what belongs to their large group and what does not.

To illustrate this let us go to the island of Cyprus, where Greeks and Turks lived side by side for centuries until the island was *de facto* divided into two political entities in 1974. Greek farmers there often raise pigs. Turkish children, like Greek children, are invariably drawn to farm animals, but imagine a Turkish child wanting to touch and love a piglet. The mother or other important individuals in the Turkish child's environment would strongly discourage the child from playing with the piglet, as, for Muslim Turks, the pig is "dirty". Accordingly, for the Turkish child the pig will be perceived as a cultural amplifier for the Greeks; it does not belong to the Turks' large group. Since Muslim Turks do not eat pork, in a concrete sense what is externalised into the image of the pig will not be reinternalised. Now the Turkish child has found a reservoir for externalising *permanently* his or her "unwanted" parts.

Let me explain what I mean by "unwanted parts". Infants and small children have loving and frustrating types of experiences when relating to their mothers and other caregivers, including "good" feeding and "bad" feeding experiences as I stated above. Much research has been done into how small children need time to integrate their "loved" and "unloved" parts and correspondingly "loving" and "frustrating" images of the mother and other persons. Some unintegrated "unwanted" aspects of their self and caretakers remain in their minds.

When small Turkish children experience a piglet as a target for externalisation of "unwanted parts", they do not fully understand what Greekness means. Sophisticated thoughts, perceptions and emotions, and images of history about the Other evolve much later without the children's awareness that *the first symbol* of the Other was in the service of helping them avoid feeling tensions due to keeping some unwanted parts within. When children find a suitable target for their "unwanted parts", the precursor of the Other becomes established in children's minds at an *experimental level*. The Other also becomes a target for prejudice, in various degrees and according to many external circumstances.

Historian Norman Itzkowitz (personal communication with author) described how some children of Polish Jewish peasant origins living in the United States, far from the dangers of the old anti-Semitic world, were taught to spit three times when passing a Catholic Church. This may be dismissed simply as superstition, but it also partakes of the notion of the church as a suitable target for externalisation. It is easier to give up "bad" targets of externalisation in an atmosphere of comparative safety, but memories of them linger on. Except those who were brought as slaves, people from different countries with different religions and other belief systems came to the United States in order to be an American and have an idealised American large-group identity. Because of this, the suitable target of externalisation to which Itzkowitz referred might not be as stable as the suitable target is for the Turkish child in Cyprus.

Unintegrated "good" images, too, find suitable targets of permanent externalisation that, as the child grows, experientially represent "we-ness" and become significant large-group identity markers. Certain cultural amplifiers, such as language, nursery rhymes, food, dances, religious symbols, or specific geographical locations become "good" targets of permanent externalisation. For example, Finnish children use the sauna for their "good" reservoir. Only when Finnish children grow up will they have sophisticated thoughts and feelings about Finnishness.

Certain historical events may increase a large group's investment in its own suitable target of externalisation. In Scotland, Highland dress dates from the thirteenth century, but it was an event in the eighteenth century that transformed the tartan kilt into a shared "good" reservoir of Scottishness. When England defeated Bonnie Prince Charlie at Culloden in 1746, the English banned the wearing of the kilt in Scotland under the Act of Proscription. The act was repealed thirty-six years later, and the kilt was adopted as Scottish military dress. When George IV made a state visit to Scotland in 1882, his visit strengthened Scottish investment in the kilt, which served to enhance Scottish "we-ness" in the face of a visit from the figurehead of powerful England. Many Scottish families even have their own tartan design, which they sometimes use in their personal clothing. Efforts to suppress the wearing of the kilt have been unsuccessful; the dress continues to serve as an ethnic reservoir signifying Scottishness.

Concepts of identification, depositing, and especially suitable targets explain humans' need to have enemies and allies in the political/social sense (Volkan, 1988). This need emanates from childhood development and is the end result of one's unavoidable efforts to find a cohesive self and to form integrated representations of others. As adults we are not aware that the beginnings of the concepts of ethnicity, nationality, or other larger-group names, as well as the concept of the enemy, are found in shared non-human and inanimate or animate objects that absorb aspects of all small children in the same large group and which are invested with emotion. At the large-group level, people need enemies to prevent aggression from turning inward in their large group (Boyer, 1986), to maintain a favourable large-group identity, and to establish peace in their large group. To have prejudices against or for another large group is a "normal" human characteristic. Prejudice may differentiate us from Others in a playful and adaptive way, or, under stressful conditions, it may become malignant.

We can now further wonder about shared prejudice against the Other. Large mammals display aggression by gesturing and making noises when they compete for food, territory, or mates; but they usually hunt and kill creatures that do not belong to their species. Chimpanzees in one group exhibit lethal aggression against chimpanzees from another group (Goodall, 1986; Mitani, Watts & Amsler, 2010). Humans surpass chimpanzees in murdering members of their own species. Throughout our history humans have exhibited *malignant* prejudices towards other human beings, hunted them, and killed them in the name of large-group identity. In order to make sense of this fact, Erikson (1966) came up with the idea that human beings have evolved, by whatever kind of evolution and for whatever adaptive reasons, into *pseudo species*, such as tribes or clans, which behave as if they were separate species. He theorised that primitive humans sought a measure of protection for their unbearable nakedness by adopting the armour of the lower animals and wearing their skins, feathers, or claws. On the basis of these outer garments, each tribe, clan, or group developed a sense of shared identity, as well as a conviction that it alone harboured *the one human identity*.

We can add another idea, also speculative, that may further explain what happened during the course of human evolution and how human large groups could kill one another while feeling that each belonged to a different species. For centuries, neighbouring tribes or clans had only each other to interact with, due to their natural boundaries. Neighbouring groups had to compete for territory, food, sex, and physical goods for their survival. Eventually, this primitive level of competition assumed more psychological implications. Physical essentials, besides retaining their status as genuine necessities, absorbed mental meanings as well, such as narcissism, competition, prestige, honour, power, envy, revenge, humiliation, submission, grief and mourning, and evolved from being tokens of survival to becoming large-group symbols, cultural amplifiers, traditions, religions, or historical memories that embedded a large group's self-esteem and identity.

Such postulations are supported by references to the Other in many ancient documents and languages. Ancient Chinese regarded themselves as *people* and viewed the Other as *kuei* or "hunting spirits". The Apache Indians considered themselves to be *indeh*, the people, and all others as *indah*, the enemy (Boyer, 1986). The Mundurucu in the Brazilian rainforest divided their world into Mundurucu, who were people, and non-Mundurucu, who were *pariwat* (enemies), except for certain neighbours whom they perceived as friendly (Murphy, 1957). Some anthropologists believe that this type of pattern cannot be literally generalised to all cultures, but it shows the communality about the sense of "otherness" and shared prejudices (Stein, 1990).

During the times about which written history is available we constantly see interactions of "pseudo species" and one group seeing the other as less than human in malignant ways: the Christian Europeans' treatment of Jews during the Middle Ages, the White Americans' treatment of African-Americans in the United States, the Nazis' behaviour, apartheid in South Africa, and more recently events such as those in the former Yugoslavia, Rwanda, and countless other places where events from human history provide examples of one large group dehumanising another. Studies in evolutionary psychology also refer to the creation of the Other and dehumanisation as elements of human nature (Smith, 2011).

To illustrate the benign, hostile, or malignant consequences of shared prejudice I came up with the tent metaphor for large groups. Think in terms of us learning to wear two main layers, like fabric, from the time we are children. The first layer, the individual layer, fits each of us snugly, like clothing. It is one's core personal identity that provides an inner sense of persistent sameness for the individual. The second layer is like the canvas of a tent, which is loose-fitting, but allows a huge number of individuals to share a sense of sameness with others under the same large-group tent. We can visualise large-group identity markers, such as specific cultural and historical images, as different colourful designs that are stitched on the canvas of each large group's metaphorical tent. Some common threads, such as identifications with intimate others in one's childhood environment, are used in the construction of both layers. Thus, the individual identity and the large-group identity, psychologically speaking, are interconnected.

Under a huge large-group tent there are subgroups and subgroup identities, such as professional and political identities. While it is the tent pole—the political leader—that holds the tent erect, the tent's canvas psychologically protects both the leader and all members of the large group. Dissenters in a large group do not change the essential shared sentiments within the large group unless they develop a huge number of followers who become a political force, an important subgroup. From an individual psychology point of view, a person may perceive the pole as a father figure and the canvas as a nurturing mother. From a large-group psychology point of view the canvas represents the large-group identity that is shared by tens or hundreds of thousands or millions of people.

Imagine two huge large-group tents standing side by side. The canvas of each tent also provides a *psychological border* for each large group. The nature of shared prejudice between the two large groups can be visualised as that which members under one tent throw at the canvas of the tent that surrounds the other large group. It may range from mud that can be washed away, to filthy waste material that sticks, to bullets that kill—shared prejudice from benign to hostile to malignant.

The psychology of international relationships is the psychology of neighbours. We still see fierce conflicts breaking out among neighbours who are in close physical proximity—for example, between Armenians and Azerbaijanis, between Tamils and Sinhalese, and between the Northern Irish Catholics and the Northern Irish Protestants. These days, now that civilisation has evolved and all parts of the world have been connected by sophisticated telecommunication systems and other technological means, all large groups are potential neighbours.

In peaceful times people attend to their families, relatives, neighbours, schools, professional and social organisations, sports clubs, local and national political parties, other subgroups, and their Facebook pages. In focusing on these routine elements of our lives we are not terribly conscious of our large-group identity—the canvas of the metaphorical tent—just as we are not usually aware of our constant breathing. If we have pneumonia or are in a burning building, we quickly notice every breath. Likewise, if the huge tent's canvas shakes or parts of it are torn apart by Others, tens, hundreds of thousands, or millions of persons under the canvas become preoccupied with it and will be emotionally ready do anything to repair, maintain, and protect it. And when they do, they are often willing to sanction extreme sadism or masochism if they think that what they are doing will help to maintain and protect their large-group identity.

The more a tent shakes or is torn apart at the hand of the Other, the more the large group under its canvas becomes obliged to hold on to its large-group identity. They may, for example, reactivate the memories of chosen traumas. This in turn will create a *time collapse*: shared anxieties, expectations, fantasies, and defences associated with the past magnify the image of the current conflicts. Large groups become psychologically willing to experience more hostile or malignant prejudice, sadistic or masochistic acts, and perpetrate monstrous cruelty against "others".

When representatives of large groups in conflict get together for unofficial diplomatic dialogues, if one side feels humiliated it reactivates its chosen traumas (usually contaminated with chosen glories). For example, during an unofficial diplomatic dialogue, while discussing current international affairs, Russians might begin to focus on the Tatar invasion, their chosen trauma. Today's extreme Muslim religious fundamentalists have reactivated numerous chosen traumas, such as losing the Caliphate when modern Turkey was born in 1923, and glories leading to time collapse. Time collapse also reactivates entitlement ideologies which accompany chosen traumas. In the next chapter I will examine these ideologies.

CHAPTER THREE

Entitlement ideologies

It is believed that the term "ideology" (science of ideas) was coined by French nobleman Antoine Louis Claude Destutt, Comte de Tracy (or briefly, Destutt de Tracy) (1754–1836) in his *Dissertation sur Quelques Questions d'Idéologie* (1799), and a series of works entitled *Projet d'Éléments d'Idéologie* (from 1801 through 1815) and related papers. This term was given currency by the rhetoricians (*les idéologues*) of the French Revolution and was read and studied by political leaders such as Thomas Jefferson—a Founding Father of the United States and the principle author of its Declaration of Independence—subsequently influencing political, economic, societal, and psychological thinking (Chinard, 1979; Scruton, 1982; Klein, 1985).

Later "ideology," as a term referring to politics, developed in many different directions. Obviously political ideologies are formulated and presented by individuals or a team of individuals, but they require a receptive large group to accept and nurture them. A political ideology sometimes appeared as systematic and all-embracing political doctrine that justified intrusion into societal and personal lives in global ways. At other times it appeared to make an impact regionally on large-group processes and, of course, on the lives of individual members of such groups, in only limited geographical areas. For example, Marxism presumed to be a universally applicable theory, while Kemalism and Gaullism referred to ideologies in Turkey and France respectively.

As the above examples indicate, political ideologies are sometimes named after persons with whom they are associated. Those interested in political science have at times hearkened back to historical figures in order to explain certain ideologies practised in the past or even in the present. For example, Calvinism as a political ideology was based on John Calvin's (1509–1564) theological system. Indeed, many political ideologies have direct or indirect origins that emerged from religious beliefs and religious understanding of human morality and rights of people as they relate to divine power (Thompson, 1980; Vasquez, 1986). But this is not always the case. Marxism, for example, is not a religiously contaminated ideology. In fact Marxism gave the term "ideology" a negative connotation, since it perceived itself as reflecting human nature. Thus, to the supporters of Marxism, "ideology is necessary only under certain social conditions (especially those of feudalism and capitalism) and … with the coming of communism, the veil of ideology will be torn aside: society and human nature will at last be perceived as they really are" (Scruton, 1982, p. 213). Nevertheless, for the rest of the world, for the "non-believers" in communism, Marxism remained a political ideology.

Obviously there are many "isms" in political science that do not carry an individual's name, but describe instead universal or regional ideological movements that become the driving force for certain political programs and actions. Besides feudalism, capitalism, and communism mentioned above, there are other examples: royalism, centrism, universalism, isolationism, Hellenism, Zionism, Pan-Islamism, Pan-Turanism (*Turan* means the land of Turkic populations), Nazism, and, of course, the most common conservatism and liberalism.

Psychoanalysts have written psychobiographies of certain political and societal leaders, such as Adolf Hitler, who evolved their own political ideologies or practised politics under the influence of certain ideologies. Usually these psychoanalytic writers' primary emphasis is on understanding leaders' internal motivations for evolving and/or practising specific ideologies. For example, in historian Norman Itzkowitz' and my detailed psychobiographical study of the life of Kemal Atatürk (1800–1938), the founder of modern Turkey, our primary focus was on the leader's internal world (Volkan & Itzkowitz, 1984). We described how the Turkish leader displaced his early image of his grieving mother (she had lost four children and a husband) onto his grieving country (after losses incurred in the Balkan Wars and the First World War) in an effort to repair the nation. "Kemalism" as a regional political ideology was one major aspect of Atatürk's attempt to repair his mother/nation. While we referred to Turks' shared massive trauma during the wars, and their loss of empire and feelings of helplessness and humiliation, we did not examine in detail the large-group processes that created an atmosphere that led the majority to accept Kemalism and modern Turkey's drastic political/cultural revolution. Our direct focus on large-group processes as they followed a shared massive trauma took place later when we examined the millennium-long Turkish-Greek relationship (Volkan & Itzkowitz, 1994). In this later study we began to observe more clearly how the shared image of ancestors' trauma at the hands of enemy Others might become the central factor in the development of political ideologies that support sadistic and/or masochistic political programs or actions in the name of exaggerated shared entitlement. I joined historian/psychoanalyst Peter Loewenberg (1991, 1995) in studying this phenomenon and came up with the term "entitlement ideology".

Loewenberg addressed the crucial bridge between massive shared trauma and historical process dominated by collective sadistic activities when he wrote about the Protestant Reformation. He states that, "[It] was a trauma of major proportions ... whose effect took centuries to work out to a new and secure equilibrium. One response of European religion, culture, and politics to these traumata was a new piety, flagellation, widespread practice of torture, and epidemics of demonic possession, which seized groups in the late fifteenth century for the first time" (p. 515).

Loewenberg described the development of a large-group process and, in a sense, a large-group ideology, that allowed the Bishop of Würzburg to kill 900 and the Bishop of Bamberg over 600. Meanwhile, in Savoy 800 were burned during a festival. He also reminded us that in this atmosphere, in 1514, 300 were executed in the small Diocese of Como.

Massive killings have obviously occurred throughout history. In examining the concept of entitlement ideology, my interest is in those tragedies that have a direct link to the shared mental representation of ancestors' trauma. The concept of *chosen trauma* illuminates the link between a trauma of major proportions at the hand of the Other and tragic events that take place some centuries later. I propose that the reactivation of a chosen trauma prepares a society to also reactivate an entitlement ideology.

In a clinical setting, according to Levin (1970), we can observe three kinds of entitlement attitudes presented by our patients. They are (a) attitudes of normal entitlement, (b) attitudes of restricted entitlement, and (c) attitudes of exaggerated entitlement. Kriegman (1988), referring to exaggerated entitlement, wrote that, "an individual may feel entitled to special privileges because of his having been an innocent victim of suffering in childhood" (p. 7). Similarly, large groups develop exaggerated entitlement because their members feel that their ancestors suffered at the hand of the Other.

Entitlement ideologies refer to a shared sense of entitlement to recover what was lost in reality and fantasy during a collective trauma that evolved as a chosen trauma and during other related shared traumas. Or they refer to the mythologised birth of a large group, a process which later generations idealise. They deny difficulties and losses that occurred during the trauma, and imagine their large group as one composed of persons belonging to an entitled superior species. Holding on to an entitlement ideology primarily reflects a complication in large-group mourning, an attempt both to deny losses as well as a wish to recover them, a narcissistic reorganisation accompanied by "bad" prejudice for the Other. Since a specific entitlement ideology becomes a specific large-group marker, paradoxically the large group may experience anxiety if a historical process is offered to end the large group's ceaseless mourning process.

Each large group's entitlement ideology is specific and is known by a specific name in the literature. What Italians call "irredentism" (related to *Italia Irredenta*) and what Greeks call "the Megali Idea" (the Great Idea) are examples of entitlement ideologies. Irredentism became a political term after the Italian nationalist movement sought annexation of lands referred to as *Italia Irredenta* (unredeemed Italy), areas inhabited by an ethnic Italian majority but under Austrian jurisdiction after 1866. The Megali Idea refers to a specific political entitlement ideology that demanded the reunification of all Greeks of the former Byzantine Empire. The Megali Idea played a significant role in Greeks' political, social, and especially religious lives, since the Greek Orthodox Church was instrumental in keeping the Megali Idea alive and active. Turks' "Pan-Turanism" (bringing all the Turkic people together from Anatolia to central Asia), Serbs' "Christoslavism" (Sells, 2002), and what extreme religious Islamists of today call "the return of an Islamic Empire" are other examples of entitlement ideology. The American entitlement ideology, usually called "American exceptionalism", was inflamed after 11 September 2001 (Hollander, 2010).

The next chapter provides a detailed example of how one chosen trauma associated with an entitlement ideology evolved and how it influenced political/societal processes.

CHAPTER FOUR

The Crusades, the fall of Constantinople, and the "Megali Idea"

Historian Norman Itzkowitz and I have studied extensively how some Christian large groups have reacted throughout the centuries to the fall of Constantinople to the Turks in 1453 and how the mental representation of this event eventually culminated in the development of a specific political entitlement ideology called "the Megali Idea" (Volkan & Itzkowitz, 1993–1994). This chapter is based on our joint study.

In 1071 AD, the Turkish Seljuk leader Sultan Alp Arslan (Heroic Lion) defeated the Byzantine forces under Emperor Romanus IV Diogenes near Manzigert in Eastern Anatolia. During the centuries following the Battle of Manzigert, Asia Minor, heartland of today's Turkey, gradually became Turkified. Soon after this battle, a group of Seljuk Turks captured Jerusalem, leading to the Crusades. By the time Crusaders entered Jerusalem, the city was no longer under Turkish occupation, but perception of the Turks as the occupiers of Christian holy land and as the enemy of Christians endured. It was, however, the fall of Constantinople to the Turks, 300 years after the Battle of Manzigert, which became a more obvious "chosen trauma" for the Christian world. Constantinople was conquered by the successors to Seljuk Turks, the Ottomans, on 29 May 1453. Historically, this marked the end of one historical era and the

39

beginning of another, as the Christian Byzantine Empire was replaced by the Moslem-dominated Ottoman Empire. Since Constantinople was taken on a Tuesday, Christians regarded every Tuesday thereafter as an unpropitious day. The seizure of Constantinople by the Turks was seen to reflect God's judgment upon "the sins of Christians everywhere" (Schwoebel, 1967, p. 14). In Europe, during medieval and early modern times, those recording historical events tended to disregard "real" causes and attribute the unfolding of human history to the hand of God. Such sentiments also appeared to some extent even after the September 11, 2001 tragedy in the United States. For example, some Christian fundamentalist groups in the US read this tragedy as divine punishment for the sinful acts of their country's homosexuals, feminists, and civil libertarians (Volkan, 2004).

In spite of the fact that Rome had refused to provide support for Constantinople against the Turks, Rome received word of Byzantium's fall with shock and disbelief. Turkish victory was seen as a knife plunged into the heart of Christianity. Aeneas Sylvius Piccolomini, a future Pope, wrote to Pope Nicholas V on 12 July 1453, that the Turks had killed Homer and Plato for the second time (Schwoebel, 1967).

The loss of Constantinople was a massive trauma that reopened wounds caused by the fall of Jerusalem, and mourning for this loss could not take place to the point of resolution or be set aside. Jerusalem had been regained and lost again, but Constantinople's fall only elicited feelings of helplessness, shame, and humiliation. The desire to undo this trauma expressed itself in rumblings about organising another Crusade. Nothing came of such talk, but the idea persisted. Together, Christians in the Ottoman territories sang the refrain "Again, with years, with time, again they will be ours," in an attempt to deny the changes that had come and to undo the losses they engendered. This would be the seed of an excessive entitlement ideology, which would be formulated later (Young, 1969).

Denial manifested in other ways as well. If a continuous link between the Turks and the Byzantines could be found, there would be less need for Byzantines and other Christians to feel pain. Many Westerners became preoccupied, sometimes in mystical ways, with the ancient origins of the Turks. For example, Giovanni Maria Filelfo, a humanist, declared that the young Turkish Sultan Mehmed II, who had seized Constantinople, was a Trojan. The German Felix Fabri studied the idea that Turks descended from Teucher, son of the Greek friend of Hercules, Telemon, and the Trojan princess Hesione. Fabri did not claim that Teucher fathered the Turks, but he held that they descended from Turcus, a son of Troyas (references to Giovanni Maria Filelfo can be found in *Monumenta Hungariae*, XXIII, part 1, no. 9, pp. 308–309, 405 and 453, and to Felix Fabri in *Evagatorium III*, pp. 236–239. See: Schwoebel, 1967).

While these pseudo-historical efforts to find continuity between the two sides continued as a way to make loss and humiliation tolerable, a counter-attempt tried to unlink them so that Byzantines could maintain their large-group identity. In Europe this led to stereotyping the Turks. According to Berkes (1964), the fates played a trick on the Turks because of their seizure of Constantinople, a notion that was condensed with a mental representation of their conquest of Jerusalem (like Seljuk Turks, Ottoman Turks also conquered Jerusalem). The Turks became the unconsciously chosen target of stubborn, systematic, and negative stereotyping by Europeans and historians throughout the West. Berkes claims that these historians never stereotyped other "strangers" such as Chinese, Arabs, and Japanese in such a way. Of course, since 11 September 2001 Arabs have become the main target of stereotyping in the United States. Indeed, after this tragedy President George W. Bush referred to the mental representation of the Crusades, echoing a "time collapse" of a Muslim-Christian clash of the past into a Muslim-Christian clash of the present.

As Europeans began discovering new regions of the world and aggressively colonising them, preoccupation with Turks as conquerors of Jerusalem and Constantinople became globalised. In 1539, for example, Mexican indigenous people took part in a dramatic pageant representing the liberation of Jerusalem from the Turks by the armies of the Catholic world joined by those from the New World (Motolinia, 1951). Even now, a variation of this pageant is still performed in Mexico, halfway around the world from Turkey (Harris, 1992). This globalised stereotyping was even incorporated into old editions of Webster's Dictionary under the definition of "Turk", which reads, "One exhibiting any quality attributed to Turks, such as sensuality and brutality." The reference to brutality is easy to understand since battles, such as the one that took place when the Turks seized Constantinople, are brutal. Itzkowitz and I (Volkan & Itzkowitz, 1994) also tried to understand the reference to sensuality. We speculated that it had a great deal to do with the youthful and virile image of Mehmed II, whose conquest was perceived as a "rape". Constantinople, which was later named Istanbul, is still experienced by today's poets as a symbol of a fallen and/or grieving woman (Halman, 1992).

Following the Greek War of Independence (1821–1832), the Greeks, heirs to Byzantium, remained "perennial mourners", unable to resolve the loss of Constantinople. As generations passed, the fall of Constantinople evolved as their major chosen trauma, and this influenced the evolution of the Megali Idea, which crystallised in the nineteenth century. Some four decades after its independence from the Ottoman Empire, the new Greek identity became a composite of Hellenic (ancient pre-Christian Greek) and Byzantine (Christian Greek) elements (Herzfeld, 1986). The urge to retain the cultural/religious elements of Byzantium was articulated through the words of such influential individuals as Spyridon Zamblios (1856, 1859) and Nikolaos G. Politis (1872, 1882). Meanwhile as Kitromilides (1990) clearly described, the nation-building process for the new Greek state gradually took on two dimensions, the first being internal—the gradual development of a nation within the independent kingdom of Greece. The other one was external and involved the influence of the Megali Idea as a point of reference for the new Greek state involving Greeks living in the Ottoman Empire in places "considered as integral parts of the historical patrimony of Hellenism" (Kitromilides, 1990, p. 35). Their Megali Idea is, "a dream shared by Greeks that someday the Byzantine Empire would be restored and all the Greek lands would once again be united into a Greater Greece" (Markides, 1977, p. 10). In order to create the Megali Idea and make it one of the emotionally charged societal motivations for Greek foreign policy, modern Greeks revived the fall of Constantinople.

It is beyond the scope of this chapter to explore fully how the Megali Idea impacted the immediate expansion of the new Greek state and the wars that took place for this purpose. Obviously, during these wars and related conflicts thousands of people were killed or injured and societies experienced terror, helplessness, and incredible grief. Also obviously, I do not reduce the causes of these wars only to the influence of the Megali Idea. I simply want to illustrate here how a political ideology of excessive entitlement becomes fuel for various infernos. One of the most recent Greek-Turkish conflicts that was fuelled by the influence of the Megali Idea in the late 1950s and early 1960s, this time on the island of Cyprus, is one with which I am most familiar. Cypriot Greek Markides (1977) wrote:

One could argue that the "Great Idea" had an internal logic, pressing
for realisation in every part of the Greek world, which continued
to be under foreign rule. Because the Greeks of Cyprus have considered themselves historically and culturally to be Greeks, the
"Great Idea" has had an intense appeal. Thus, when the church
fathers called on the Cypriots [Cypriot Greeks] to fight for union
with Greece, it did not require much effort to heat up emotions ...
Enosis [Uniting Cyprus with Greece] did not originate in the church
but in the minds of intellectuals in their attempt to revive Greek-
Byzantine civilisation. However, being the most central and
powerful of institutions, the church contributed immensely to its
development. The church embraced the movement and for all
practical purposes became its guiding nucleus. (pp. 10–11)

It appears, however, that since Greece became a member of the
European Union the impact of the Megali Idea on Greek foreign policy
has lost its strong appeal. However, it is very difficult for a large group
to "forget" a shared political ideology that is connected with a chosen
trauma. This is because of the conscious and unconscious shared tasks,
mentioned earlier, that chosen traumas incorporate. In April 2004 two
referenda took place in Cyprus. Both Greek and Turkish sides voted to
accept or reject a kind of "reunification". (Since 1974 the island has been
divided into northern Turkish and southern Greek sectors.) The Greek
side overwhelmingly voted against such a "reunification". Under a
United Nations plan, Cyprus (now only the Greek side) would become
a member of the European Union on 1 May 2004. There are many *realpolitik* causes for Cypriot Greeks voting "no". But their decision was
also influenced by the Megali Idea. Before the referendum the Greek
Orthodox Church on the island preached that any Cypriot Greek voting "yes" would go to Hell. The Cypriot Greeks "illusion" to posses the
whole island (Megali Idea) prevailed over the idea of a kind of "togetherness" with the Cypriot Turks.

My aim in this chapter is to illustrate, basically from a historical point
of view, the relations between a large group's ancestor's massive trauma
and how it creates an atmosphere for the development of an exaggerated entitlement ideology. I should repeat: I would by no means want to
reduce Greek-Turkish relations to the impact of the Megali Idea alone.
I do not wish to give the impression that in international relations only
one side's issues cause trouble and violence. Usually reasons for the

violence originate from both sides. But, for the purpose of this chapter, I have focused only on one theme—the concept of trauma at the hand of the Other and its relationship to an ideology.

We have studied the long-term effects of ancestors' traumas at the hand of the Other, concepts of chosen trauma and entitlement ideology and the significant roles they play in defining large-group identity. In the next chapter I will examine psychological processes and societal shifts following a massive trauma caused by an enemy. I will focus on traumatised large groups.

CHAPTER FIVE

Traumatised large groups, societal shifts, and transgenerational transmissions

W hen a massive disaster occurs, those who are affected will experience its psychological impact in three different ways. First, many individuals will suffer from various forms of post-traumatic stress problems. Second, new social processes and shared behaviours will appear throughout the affected large group. And third, traumatised persons will, mostly unconsciously, oblige their progeny to resolve the directly traumatised generation's own unfinished psychological tasks related to the shared trauma (transgenerational transmissions). This chapter focuses on the latter two expressions of disasters' psychological impact, particularly in situations when shared trauma occurs at the hand of the Other.

Shared catastrophes are of various types. Some result from natural causes, such as tropical storms, floods, volcanic eruptions, forest fires, earthquakes, or tsunamis. Some are accidental manmade disasters, like the 1986 Chernobyl accident which spewed tons of radioactive dust into the atmosphere. Sometimes, the death of a leader, or of a person who also functions as a "transference figure" for most members of the large group, creates individualised as well as societal responses—for example, the assassinations of John F. Kennedy (Wolfenstein & Kliman, 1965) or Martin Luther King in the United States and Yitzhak Rabin in Israel (Erlich, 1998; Raviv, Sadeh, Raviv, Silberstein & Diver, 2000; Moses-Hrushovski, 2000), or the deaths of the American astronauts and teacher Christa McAuliffe in the 1986 space shuttle Challenger explosion (Volkan, 1997). The murders of Giorgi Chanturia in the Republic of Georgia and Rafik Hariri in Lebanon were also traumatic for large groups. There are countless examples from many locations of the world. Other shared experiences of disaster are due to the deliberate actions of an enemy ethnic, national, religious, or ideological large group. Such intentional catastrophes range from terrorist attacks to genocide, and from the traumatised large group actively fighting its enemy to the traumatised large group rendered passive and helpless.

Even though they may cause massive environmental destruction as well as societal grief, anxiety, and change, natural or accidental disasters should, generally speaking, be differentiated from those in which the catastrophe is due to ethnic or other large-group conflicts. When nature shows its fury and people suffer, victims tend ultimately to accept the event as fate or as the will of God (Lifton & Olson, 1976). After manmade accidental disasters, survivors may blame a small number of individuals or governmental organisations for their carelessness, but even then there are no Others who have *intentionally* hurt the victims. When a trauma results from war, terrorism, or other ethnic, national, religious, or ideological conflict, however, there is an identifiable enemy large group that has deliberately inflicted pain, suffering, and helplessness on its victims. Such trauma affects large-group identity issues in ways entirely different from the effects of natural or accidental disasters.

It is sometimes difficult to categorise a disaster. For instance, the massive August 1999 earthquake in Turkey that killed an estimated 20,000 people was, of course, a natural disaster. But it is also an example of a manmade accidental catastrophe because many of the structures that collapsed during the earthquake had not been built according to appropriate standards. Furthermore, it became known after the quake, that builders had bribed certain local authorities in order to construct cheaper, unsafe buildings. Incidentally, among the most interesting effects of the quake was that the disaster stimulated changes in heretofore durable ethnic sentiments. After the earthquake, rescue workers from many nations rushed to Turkey to help—Greeks among them. By publishing individual pictures and stories of Greek rescue workers, Turkish newspapers helped to induce wide-range appreciation for the Greeks as a large group. For decades they had generally been perceived as an "enemy". Indeed, only a few years before the quake, Turkey and Greece had almost gone to war in a dispute over some rocks (Kardak/ Imia) near Turkish shores (Volkan, 1997). The Turkish disaster and the earthquake in Greece the following month actually initiated a new relationship between the two nations—what was referred to in many diplomatic circles as "earthquake diplomacy".

A study comparing Armenians directly affected by the 1988 Armenian earthquake with Armenians traumatised as a result of Armenian-Azerbaijan ethnic enmities during the same year concludes that, after eighteen months and again after fifty-four months, there were no significant differences in individual "PTSD (post-traumatic stress disorder) severity ... between subjects exposed to severe earthquake trauma versus those exposed to severe violence" (Goenjian et al., 2000, p. 911). Such statistical studies measuring observable manifestations of a trauma's lasting effects (anxiety, depression, or other signs of post-traumatic stress) may be misleading, however, insofar as they do not tell us much about individual minds or hidden, internal psychological processes; apparent symptomatic uniformity may hide significant qualitative differences. Further, such studies do not tell us about societal processes that may result from catastrophes. For instance, the fact that many injured Armenians refused to accept blood donated by Azerbaijanis after the earthquake indicates that the tragedy had in fact enhanced ethnic sentiments, including resistance to "mixing blood" (symbolising large-group identity) with the enemy.

All types of massive disasters have psychological repercussions beyond individual post-traumatic stress problems. Indeed, the fact that natural or manmade disasters evoke societal responses has long been known. If the "tissues" of the community (Erikson, 1975) are not broken, however, the society eventually recovers in what Williams and Parkes (1975) refer to as a process of "biosocial regeneration" (p. 304). For example, for five years following the deaths of 116 children and twenty-eight adults in an avalanche of coal slurry in the Welsh village of Aberfan in 1966, there was a significant increase in the birthrate among women who had not themselves lost a child.

The impact of some accidental manmade disasters is much wider. Again, the nuclear accident at Chernobyl, with at least 8,000 deaths (including thirty-one killed instantly), provides a representative example. Anxiety about radiation contamination lasted many years, and with good reason. But these fears exercised a considerable impact on the social fabric of communities in and around Chernobyl. Thousands in neighbouring Belarus, for example, considered themselves contaminated with radiation and did not wish to have children, fearing birth defects. Thus the existing norms for finding a mate, marrying, and planning a family were significantly disrupted. Those who did have children often remained continually anxious that something "bad" would appear in their children's health. Here, instead of an adaptive "biosocial regeneration", society reacted with what might be termed a "biosocial degeneration".

"Biosocial regeneration" and "degeneration" are also observable after disasters due to ethnic or other large-group hostilities. A somewhat *indirect* "biosocial regeneration" occurred among Cypriot Turks during the six-year period (1963–1968) in which they were forced by Cypriot Greeks to live in ethnic enclaves confined to only three per cent of the island, under subhuman conditions. Though they were massively traumatised, their "backbone" was not broken because of the hope that the motherland, Turkey, would come to their aid. Instead of bearing increased numbers of children like the inhabitants of Aberfan, they raised hundreds and hundreds of parakeets in cages (parakeets are not native to Cyprus)—representing the "imprisoned" Cypriot Turks. As long as the birds sang and reproduced, the Cypriot Turks' anxiety remained under control (Volkan, 1979a). The art and literature stemming from the Hiroshima tragedy (Lifton, 1968) might also be considered a form of symbolic biosocial regeneration. In the case of Hiroshima, however, the society also exhibited "biosocial degeneration" and showed "death imprints" for decades after the catastrophe; the society's "backbone" was in fact broken, and biosocial regeneration could only be limited and sporadic.

Although massive disasters may sometimes fall into several categories at once, and individualised post-traumatic symptoms may be alike even when they are due to various types of massive trauma, it remains useful to consider catastrophes of different types. This is because those that are due to ethnic, national, religious, or ideological conflicts—including wars, war-like situations, and terrorism—are the only kinds that can trigger specific initial large-group identity problems as well as years, or decades, of large-group identity processes as described in the previous chapters.

When a large group's conflict with the Other becomes inflamed, the bonding between members belonging to the same large group intensifies. There is a shift in members' narcissistic investments in their large-group identity; under stressful conditions, large-group identity may supersede individual identity. The relationships between people in two opposing large groups become governed absolutely by two obligatory principles:

1. Maintaining a *psychological border* between the two large groups at any cost
2. Keeping the large-group identity separate from the identity of the enemy.

When there is anxiety and regression within neighbouring large groups in conflict, physical borders are successful only when they represent a sufficient psychological one. The physical border is perceived as a clear separation between the two large groups, allowing the illusion of a contamination-free gap between them. This gap also stabilises one large group's externalisations and projections onto the other large group.

In the example that follows, we see how a symbolic psychological border was created and how one group protected its identity from being contaminated with the Other's large-group identity. After the Turkish army came to Cyprus and the island was divided into northern Turkish and southern Greek sections in 1974, the Cypriot Turks escaping from the south were placed in Cypriot Greek homes in villages vacated by the Greeks who had escaped to the south. During the first winter after these massive forced migrations took place, the northern Turkish authorities provided blankets for the new Turkish settlers. Inexplicably, the new Cypriot Turkish settlers soon began *burning the blankets* even though, logically, they needed them to keep warm.

An examination of these actions revealed that since the Cypriot Turks believed that the blankets were made from cloth left behind by the Cypriot Greeks, they unconsciously did not wish the symbolic images of their enemies to touch their bodies. This was their main psychological reason for burning the blankets, along with guilt feelings for living in the vacated houses of the enemy.

When large groups are not the "same", and when a psychological border is firmly established, each can project more effectively its unwanted aspects onto the enemy, thereby sometimes even "dehumanising" (Bernard, Ottenberg & Redl, 1973) that enemy to varying degrees. After the acute phase of the catastrophe ends, however, these two principles may remain operational for years or decades. Anything that disturbs them brings massive anxiety, and large groups may feel entitled to do anything to preserve the principles of absolute differentiation—which, in turn, protects their large-group identity. Thus, hostile interactions are perpetuated. When one large group victimises another, those who are traumatised do not typically turn to "fate" or "God" to understand and assimilate the effects of the tragedy as they would after a natural disaster. Instead, they may experience an increased sense of rage and entitlement to revenge. If circumstances do not allow them to express their rage, it may turn into a "helpless rage"—a sense of victimisation links members of the group and enhances their sense of "we-ness". We see the tragic results of this cycle across the globe.

A large group traumatised at the hand of the Other needs to grasp onto its traditional societal/cultural customs in order to protect and maintain its large-group identity and differentiate it from the enemy's large-group identity. However, since the members of the large group are helpless, humiliated and angry, and are suffering from complicated mourning due to various types of losses, enhanced or reactivated traditional social/cultural customs do not look exactly like the original ones; they are now linked with aggression turned inward, and some of their aspects are exaggerated. This situation may in turn initiate shifts in social customs.

In the early 1990s, after the collapse of the Soviet Union and the establishment of the Republic of Georgia, bloody fights took place between ethnic Georgians and ethnic South Ossetians living within the same legal/political boundary of the Republic of Georgia. In fact, South Ossetians declared their own "independent state". I studied societal changes in South Ossetia for five years, starting four years after the war (Volkan, 2006a, 2013). I learned that since the war the gender balance of the workforce had changed drastically in South Ossetia because many men had gone away to find jobs elsewhere, usually in parts of the Russian Federation. Women had to work outside the home to earn enough to feed their children and themselves, for example, by opening market stands. But, according to tradition, a woman who worked with the public was considered to be a "loose" woman. When husbands came back, some of them physically abused their wives.

There was another societal shift, a tragic one, also connected to gender issues, which was directly related to a reactivated social custom.

Part of traditional South Ossetian culture included the ritual of a young man "kidnapping" a young girl—with the knowledge of the families—and then marrying her. After the brutal war and ensuing economic and political turmoil in the late 1990s and early 2000s, the traditional "kidnapping" reappeared in a more sinister fashion. The "kidnappings" became more haphazard and were carried out with aggression, often accompanied by rape; frequently they did not end in marriage. When I interviewed young persons and their families I learned that both young men and women were trying to be "real" South Ossetians when they created big emotional and realistic problems for themselves and their families. Because of the societal dysfunction and the area's economic collapse, many girls also turned to prostitution. This in turn set in motion a new cultural phenomenon: men began marrying younger and younger women. In a culture where a bride's virginity was crucial, the notion was that the younger the bride, the more likely she was to still be virginal.

The following examples of societal shift come from Kuwait three years after the country's liberation in February 1991. W. Nathaniel Howell had been US ambassador to Kuwait and had kept the embassy open for seven months during the Iraqi occupation of Kuwait City. Under his directorship, a Center for the Study of Mind and Human Interaction (CSMHI) team made three diagnostic visits to Kuwait in 1993. We interviewed more than 150 people from diverse social backgrounds and ages to learn how the mental representation of the shared disaster echoed in their internal worlds. The technique used was based on psychoanalytic clinical diagnostic interviews, in which the analyst "hears" the subject's internal conflicts, defences, and adaptations. As the subject reports fantasies and dreams, this material adds to the interviewer's understanding of the interviewee's internal world. As can easily be imagined, we found that many Kuwaitis suffered from undiagnosed individual post-stress problems. Nevertheless, our emphasis in these interviews was not on individual diagnosis, but on discovering shifts in societal conventions and processes. After interview data was collected we looked for common themes indicating shared perceptions, expectations, and defences against conflicts created by the traumatic event (Howell, 1993, 1995; Saathoff, 1995–1996; Volkan, 1997, 2013).

Three years after Saddam Hussein's forces were driven out of Kuwait we noted that young Kuwaiti men became hesitant to marry. Those engaged to be married began postponing their marriages. This changed a well-established traditional social/cultural marriage custom in Kuwait. We wondered why.

Many whom my colleagues and I interviewed in Kuwait three years after the liberation told us a joke about "stupid" Iraqis who did not know the difference between animals, especially which ones are eatable and which are not. In the joke the Iraqis open the cages at the zoo in Kuwait City and eat inedible animals. When I first heard this joke I did not yet know the story of how the invading Iraqi soldiers had put a Kuwaiti woman in a cage.

Here is an eye-witness account of this story by a Kuwaiti man who was a member of a resistance force:

> On February 26, with the liberation, we were told that a Kuwaiti woman had been taken into the zoo grounds by the Iraqis. There were so many stories in the chaos, it was hard to know. But we kept hearing this story again and again. After four days we went to the zoo. What I saw, I will never forget: a naked woman was there in a cage. I cannot describe her body, she was so bruised, but she was still alive.
>
> In the cage she acted like an animal, moving around madly on her hands and feet. I tried to calm her, saying, "Look, we are free now, we have come to help you." I laid down my rifle to show her I meant no harm, but she became more agitated. She could not be calm, and acted angrier, upset and like an animal. I talked to my captain and we agreed that we could not let her out of the cage since she was not in her right mind. We decided to wait with her until the proper people arrived to take her to a psychiatric hospital. Remembering these events still disturbs me terribly. I cannot get them out of my mind.

When I learned the story I came to the conclusion that this woman's horrible fate and the Iraqis' inability to differentiate between a human being and an animal stimulated the content of the popular joke. People knew about the woman in a cage, but had difficulty talking about it openly. Shame and anxiety about what had happened in the zoo were covered up by the storyline of the joke, reversing horror and turning it to laughter.

In 1993 and 1994, our interviews revealed that the idea of a Kuwaiti woman being abused sexually in such an unimaginable way combined with many other horror stories about raped women, including some young Kuwaiti men being forced at gunpoint to have sex with their sisters while Iraqis watched, had created a shared "psychic reality". In this "psychic truth" all Kuwaiti women, especially from the younger generation, were *unconsciously* tainted. This unconscious "reality" was generalised and settled in the minds of Muslim Kuwaiti males. This is why many young Kuwaiti men spoke openly about postponing their marriages. I noted that this was due to the unconscious "psychic reality" that every young woman in Kuwait might no longer be a virgin. According to social/cultural custom young Muslim Kuwaiti males would not consider marrying a young woman who was tainted. Kuwaiti men needed to hold on to their large-group identity.

We found other expressions of societal shift in post-liberation Kuwait which are not directly related to grasping onto large-group identity, but they are directly related to trauma at the hand of the Other. During the invasion and occupation, many Kuwaiti fathers were humiliated in front of their children by Iraqi soldiers, who sometimes spat on Kuwaiti men, beat them, or otherwise rendered them helpless before their children's eyes. In cases where humiliation or torture had occurred away from their children's view, the fathers often wanted to hide what had happened to them. Without necessarily being aware of it, fathers began to distance themselves from certain crucial emotional interactions with their children, especially with their sons, in order to hide or to deny their sense of shame. Most children and adolescents, nevertheless, "knew" what had happened to their fathers, whether they had personally witnessed it or not.

Many school buildings in Kuwait City were used as torture chambers during the Iraqi occupation. When I visited Kuwait City during this project, however, it was hard to believe from looking at schools and other buildings that catastrophe had struck there only three years earlier; except for several buildings with bullet holes intentionally left as they were as "memorials", the rest of the city appeared completely renovated. Adults did not speak to the children about what had happened in the schools during the invasion, but the children knew; and, when they returned to these schools, that "secret" quite naturally caused them psychological problems. The very young—without, of course, knowing why—began to identify with Saddam Hussein instead of with their own fathers. In one telling instance at an elementary school play staging the story of the Iraqi invasion, the children applauded enthusiastically for the youngster who played the role of Saddam Hussein (Saathoff, 1996). "Identification with the aggressor" is the psychoanalytic term for a period in which a child identifies with the parent of the same sex with whom the child has been involved in a competition for the affection of the parent of the opposite sex (A. Freud, 1936). In childhood, this process results in a child's emotional growth. A little boy, for example, through identification with his father, whom he perceives as an "aggressor", makes a kind of entrance into manhood himself. In other situations however, like those of many Kuwaiti elementary school children, identification with the aggressor—in this case, Saddam Hussein—could create problems.

The reiteration of the "distant father" scenario in Kuwaiti families thus set in motion new processes across Kuwaiti society. Many male children who needed to identify with their fathers on the way to developing their own manhood responded poorly to the distance between themselves and their fathers—resulting, for example, in gang formations among teenagers. Frustrated by the distant and humiliated fathers (and mothers) who would not talk to their sons about the traumas of the invasion, they linked themselves together and expressed their frustrations by joining gangs. Of course, a type of "gang" formation is a normal process of the adolescent passage, as youngsters loosen their internal ties to the images of important persons of their childhood and expand their social and internal lives through investment in "new" object images as well as in members of their peer group. In the ordinary course of events, however, this "second individuation" (Blos, 1979) maintains an internal continuity with the youngster's childhood investments. For example, the "new" investment in the image of a movie star is unconsciously connected with the "old" investment in the image of the oedipal mother; or, a "new" investment in a friend remains somewhat connected to the "old" image of a sibling or other relative. Humiliated and helpless parent-images necessarily complicated the unconscious relationship between the Kuwaiti youngsters' "new" and "old" investments. Indeed, as we have also found in other situations, when many parents are affected by a catastrophe inflicted by Others, the adolescent gangs that form after the acute phase of the shared trauma tend to be more pathological. In Kuwait, the new gangs were heavily involved in car theft—a new social process and emergence of a crime that essentially had not existed in pre-invasion Kuwait.

Based on our research, the CSMHI team suggested to Kuwaiti authorities a number of political and educational strategies to help their society mourn its losses and changes, and speak openly about the helplessness and humiliation of the occupation. These would be carried out in a way that would heal splits between generations as well as between subgroups within Kuwaiti society, such as between those who fought against the Iraqis directly and those who escaped from Kuwait and returned after the invasion was over. When we presented our findings about children and adolescents in a tactful manner to the authorities, however, Kuwaiti funding for the project stopped abruptly. It seems that, for political reasons, maintaining a shared denial was preferable to the systematic and therapeutic reopening of Kuwaitis' psychological "wounds" in order for them to heal in a more adaptive manner. Also, I sensed that the Kuwaiti's increased narcissistic investment in their large-group identity made it very hard for them to receive "suggestions" from a foreign team. I do not have direct observations about the outcome of these societal changes in Kuwait as years passed. However, some observations of Kuwait of today are presented in my book *Enemies on the Couch* (Volkan, 2013).

I believe that non-governmental organisations (NGOs)—and those foreign psychiatrists, psychologists, social workers, or occasionally psychoanalysts associated with them—can mitigate maladaptive societal shifts directly related to large-group identity issues and/or traumatic events due to the enemy's activities by improving the caretaking skills of indigenous mental health workers in two ways. First, they can train these local caregivers through lectures, seminars, and workshops. In the course of CSMHI's work in traumatised societies such as Northern Cyprus, Kuwait, the former Yugoslavia, and the Republic of Georgia, after bloody events, I have concluded that NGOs have been most helpful in providing this intellectual, consultative, and supervisory help to local healthcare workers. It is not an easy task, indeed, since there may be few, if any, previously trained psychiatrists, psychologists, or similar professionals in a given area.

Providing intellectual support, however, is not enough. I propose that, to be truly helpful, foreign mental health workers, especially those with psychodynamic insights, must consider a second, concurrent approach, one that is often bypassed in most affected areas: outside experts must, from the first, pay attention to local mental health workers' own psychological needs. Without working out their own internal conflicts concerning ethnic or other large-group conflicts, indigenous workers will not be fully able to help their own people and interfere with maladaptive societal shifts however high the quality of the consultative and supervisory aid they receive from foreign workers.

I met one Bosnian psychiatrist who, having survived the 1993 siege of Sarajevo, found herself "paralysed" in the work of treating the traumatised population when peace finally arrived. The months-long siege by Bosnian Serbs was a massive catastrophe in itself. About 11,000 residents of Sarajevo were killed and an estimated 61,000 were wounded. Everyone, including mental health workers, was traumatised. Three years before I met her, this psychiatrist had begun to experience a symptom that she continued to have when our paths crossed: before going to sleep or upon awakening, she would check her legs to see if they were still attached to her body. When I examined the meaning of the symptom with her, we discovered that it was connected to an incident during the siege. She had rushed to the hospital one night, fearing that she might be shot by a stray bullet, and had seen there a young Bosnian man whom she had known before the ethnic troubles began. The young man's legs had been smashed in a bomb explosion, and they had to be amputated, an operation that she witnessed. This incident, for personal psychological reasons, came to symbolise the tragedy of Sarajevo for her. Unconsciously, she identified with this young man. Instead of recalling the tragedy by experiencing appropriate emotions, she was remembering only her own horror of being under enemy attack, day after day. Because of her unconscious fear of experiencing these terrible feelings, she could not fully help her patients experience their emotions in the therapeutic setting, or relieve them of maladaptively repressing or denying what had happened to them. A few months after I brought the connection between her symptom and her identification with the young man to her attention, however, her symptoms disappeared.

In bloody ethnic or other large-group conflicts, those who are not directly affected are also psychologically affected by the large group's trauma. Under these circumstances, even a person who is in no way directly affected tends to experience feelings in common with the other members of the large group—ranging from group pride and a sense of revenge-entitlement to large-group shame and humiliation and helplessness. These are inherently collective feelings; the loss of people, land, and prestige affects everyone in a victimised large group—including indigenous mental health caregivers.

When a traumatised large group cannot reverse its feelings of helplessness and humiliation, cannot assert itself, cannot effectively go through the work of mourning, and cannot complete other psychological journeys, it transfers these unfinished psychological tasks to future generations. During recent decades, the mental health community has learned much about the transgenerational transmission of shared trauma and its relation to the mental health of future generations. Nevertheless, this mental health issue has not received sufficient consideration from those official international organisations and NGOs that deal with the psychological wellbeing of refugees, internally displaced individuals, and others who have experienced the horrors of wars or war-like conditions. For example, most manuals of organisations such as the World Health Organization (WHO) and the Office of the United Nations High Commissioner for Refugees (UNHCR) on the mental health of refugees mention crisis intervention methods, relaxation techniques, how to deal with alcohol and drug problems, and professional conduct towards rape victims. Of course, after a disaster, the crisis situation takes precedence over other considerations, but, when the crisis is over, crucial psychological processes continue in full force. Such reports do not refer at all to the serious issues of societal response and transgenerational transmission following ethnic, national, religious, or ideological conflicts.

If we want to understand the tenacity of large-group conflict at the hand of the Other, we must understand further the mechanisms of transgenerational transmission. One of the best-known examples of a relatively simple form of transgenerational transmission comes from Anna Freud and Dorothy Burlingham's (1942) observations of women and children during the Nazi attacks on London. Freud and Burlingham noted that infants under three did not become anxious during the bombings unless their mothers were afraid. There is, as later studies have established, fluidity between a child's "psychic borders" and those of the mother and other caretakers, and the child–mother/caretaker experiences generally function as a kind of "incubator" for the child's developing mind. Besides growth-initiating elements, however, the caretaker from the older generation can also transmit undesirable psychological elements to the child.

The same fluidity can also occur in adults under certain conditions of regression, such as after massive shared catastrophes, even after the crisis situation ends and life as refugees, for example, begins. At a location near Tbilisi, Georgia, I examined a Georgian woman in her early forties from Abkhazia and her sixteen-year-old daughter who had been refugees for over four years. The two were living with other family members under miserable conditions in a refugee camp. Every night, the mother went to bed worrying about how to feed her three teenage children the next day. She never spoke to her only daughter about her concerns, but the girl sensed her mother's worry and unconsciously developed a behaviour to respond to and alleviate her mother's pain. The daughter refused to exercise, became somewhat obese, and wore a frozen smile on her face. As I interviewed both of them, I learned that the daughter, through her bodily symptoms, was trying to send her mother this message: "Mother, don't worry about finding food for your children. See, I am already overfed and happy!"

There are various forms of transgenerational transmission. Besides anxiety, depression, elation, or worries such as those the Georgian woman from Abkhazia presented, one person may "deposit" injured self-images—and sometimes even the images of the perpetrators—into the self of a child and "assign" the child psychological tasks. It is this transgenerational conveyance of long-lasting tasks that perpetuates the cycle of societal trauma described in the previous chapters. In the next chapter I will examine what I mean by large-group regression—as well as large-group progression.

CHAPTER SIX

Large-group regression and progression

When a large-group identity is threatened after a massive trauma at the hand of the Other or by other events, such as revolutions or newly gained independence, during which a large group asks "Who are we now?" we can consider this large group to be in a regressed state. I borrow the term "regression" from individual psychology because I do not have a word that stands only for large-group regression. This issue needs some explanation. Individuals are capable of individuating adaptively and moving up to levels where they utilise more sophisticated psychological capabilities that keep their less sophisticated ones in the shadows and harmless. In individual regression we say that a "normal" person, due to an external trauma or an internal one such as an anxiety-creating nightmare, psychologically goes back and utilises more "primitive" mental mechanisms like internalisation and externalisation of self—and object images, introjections and projection of thoughts or affects, fragmentation, splitting, disassociation, and denial to deal with the external world. On the other hand, large groups, especially while dealing with large-group identity issues, even in "normal" times extensively utilise primitive mechanisms and are always ready to hold on to prejudicial conceptions about other large groups and "swallow" propaganda about their own superiority.

In other words, when a large group "goes back", its regression starts from an already regressed position. We can say that politics and diplomacy are in the service of stabilising "normal" large-group regression (Volkan, 2004). For this reason I am searching for a better word to describe societal regression. I will use "societal disorganisation" and "societal regression" interchangeably. Perhaps Hopper's (2003) term "societal incohesion" is better. More important than finding the proper term however, is understanding the concept of large-group regression/ disorganisation itself.

There are typical signs of large-group regression, and I will describe these in the text that follows. Since large groups as I describe them in this book have their own specific characteristics which are built upon a centuries-old continuum and shared mental representation of history and myth, the examination of signs and symptoms of their regression should also include psychological processes that are *specific* to such large groups. In order to communicate with diplomats and others who must deal with international conflicts, clinicians need to go beyond a *general* description of the emergence of "bad" prejudice and aggression in large groups when they regress, and their shared paranoid or narcissistic sentiments, and refer to actual manifestations of regression within each specific large group.

In the previous chapter, referring to societal/cultural customs, I illustrated how a regressed large group wants to grasp on to its *large-group identity markers*. Metaphorically speaking, the large group repaints such identity designs on the canvas of the large-group tent in order to show that its identity still survives and to ease shared anxiety. I also stated that new paintings may look different due to societal shifts. The large group, however, also exhibits, in an exaggerated way, its flag and other items that openly show the members' shared narcissistic investment in their large-group identity.

Another sign of large-group regression, *rallying around the leader*—as occurred in the United States immediately following the 11 September 2001 terrorist attacks—has been known since Freud. When Freud (1921c) wrote about this phenomenon however, he did not say that he was referring to regressed groups (Waelder, 1930). Sometimes the members of a large group continue to rally around a leader for decades and remain "regressed" in order to modify the existing characteristics of their large-group identity. In this situation, what we observe is similar to an individual's regression in the service of progression and creativity. After the collapse of the Ottoman Empire, the people of Turkey, in general, continued to rally around Kemal Atatürk (the leader of modern Turkey which was established in 1923) until his death in 1938 (Volkan & Itzkowitz, 1984). This was the main element that supported modern Turkey's cultural revolution and the modification of characteristics of the Turks' large-group identity. On the other hand, in certain totalitarian regimes, people rally around the leader in order to feel personal security rather than be punished. Without being aware of it, they internalise what Šebek (1994) called *totalitarian objects*, and blindly follow their leader by giving up many aspects of their individuality.

Two types of splitting also signal large-group regression. First, a splitting between "us" and "them" (the enemy outside the regressed large group) becomes very strong, and the Other becomes a target for dehumanisation (Bernard, Ottenberg & Redl, 1973). Second, in regressed large groups, following the initial rallying around the leader, a severe split occurs within the large group itself when the leader cannot differentiate where real danger ends and where the fantasised danger begins, when the leader cannot maintain hope or tame shared aggression. The shared feeling of "basic trust" within the large group will then be lost. The term *basic trust*, first described by Erikson (1956), is a concept that describes how children learn to feel comfortable putting their own safety in a caretaker's hands; by developing basic trust, children discover in turn how to trust themselves. If a child cannot trust his mother and father, then he will have difficulty trusting himself. In large groups when there is no severe regression, members in their routine daily lives maintain their basic trust and in turn they associate with other members without discomfort.

Members of a large group go along with their leaders in reactivating *chosen glories* and *chosen traumas* with good or malignant consequences. When a large group is in a regressed state, the personality and the internal world of the political leader assumes great importance concerning the manipulation (the "good" or the "bad") of what already exists within the large-group psychology.

During the Gulf War Saddam Hussein depended heavily on chosen glories to galvanise the Iraqi people's support, even associating himself with Sultan Saladin who defeated the Christian Crusaders in the twelfth century. By reviewing a past event and a historic hero, Saddam aimed to create the illusion that a similar triumphal destiny was awaiting his people and that he, like Saladin, was a hero. Saddam, like Saladin, was born in Tikrit, but it did not matter to Saddam that he had ruled from Egypt rather than Iraq, or that Saladin was not an Arab but a Kurd—in fact, Saddam had killed many Iraqi Kurds. The emphasis was principally on the ancient's hero's religious large-group identity. Often, chosen glories and chosen traumas are intertwined.

In regressed large groups political, legal, or traditional *borders* begin to symbolise the canvas of the large-group tent. In other words, borders become highly psychologised and people, leaders, and official organisations become preoccupied with their protection. Since there is a realistic danger "out there", obviously borders need to be protected, and because of this, it is difficult to study the psychological aspects of this preoccupation. When I was an inaugural Rabin Fellow at the Yitzhak Rabin Center for Israeli Studies in Tel Aviv during the spring of 2001, I had a chance to study and describe the border psychology in Israel at close range (Volkan, 2004). In the United States and almost everywhere in the world, especially since 11 September 2001, we are subjected almost daily to the influence of border psychology. At airports, for example, we deny the assault on our individual autonomy at the security checkpoints because of the possibility of real danger, and subject ourselves to large-group psychology; our individual psychology that prompts us to rebel against the intrusion from outside is relegated to the background.

In *Taboo of Virginity* Freud (1918a) coined the phrase "narcissism of minor differences" to describe the way individuals divide and delineate from one another in human relationships. Later, in 1930, he referred to communities with adjoining territories that "are engaged in constant feuds and in ridiculing each other—like the Spaniards and the Portuguese, for instance, the North Germans and the South Germans, the English and Scotch, and so on". He added: "I gave this phenomenon the name of 'the narcissism of minor differences', a name which does not do much to explain it. We can see that it is a convenient and relatively harmless satisfaction of the inclination to aggression, by means of which cohesion between members of the community is made easier" (1930a, p. 114). When a large group's tent canvas is attacked and torn apart, minor differences between enemy groups become major issues, even deadly ones, since minor differences are experienced as unchangeable "borders" separating one large group's identity from their enemy's identity (Volkan, 1988, 1997, 2006a).

Many symbols that mark large-group identities have played a role in accentuating minor differences. For example, the inhabitants of Andhra Pradesh in India often wear neck scarves, whereas members of the neighbouring group with whom they sometimes fight, the Telanganas, do not. Between regressed Croats and Serbs, dialect differences—such as the Croat *mlijeko* (milk) versus the Serb *mleko*—carried a heavy political-cultural load during the conflicts between these two large groups. In times of stress and violent outbreaks, identifying minor differences may have deadly implications. Sinhalese mobs in the Sri Lankan riots of 1958, for example, relied on a variety of subtle indicators—such as the presence of earring holes in the ear or the manner in which a shirt was worn—to identify their enemy Tamils, whom they then attacked or killed (Horowitz, 1985).

A regression within the large group stimulates and increases the population's sharing of primitive mental mechanisms in dealing with the external world. I am referring to massive *internalisations* of object images/*introjections* of ideas and affects. These may be such things as the population "eating up" political propaganda without making much of an effort to analyse whether what is coming into their inner world is poisonous or not, or massive *externalisations* of unwanted self— and object images/*projections* of unacceptable thoughts and affects, such as happened under the totalitarian regime of Enver Hoxha. At that time, Albanians created a dangerous enemy image and then built 7,500 bunkers throughout Albania in anticipation of an attack by this "enemy". Building these bunkers, which in reality would never withstand modern weaponry, was also a reflection of *magical thinking*, another symptom of large-group regression. Within regressed societies we see various types of shared magical thinking, often expressed with an expansion of religious fundamentalist thinking.

Lastly, I want to describe what I call *purification*, which stands for a process also initiated by shared externalisations and projections. After a massive trauma at the hand of enemies, and after the reactivation of chosen traumas and glories—in short, after questioning a shift in large-group identity—a large group shakes its canvas to get rid of unwanted elements like a snake sheds its skin. In my view, this is an obligatory process. The process of purification occurs on a spectrum, from getting rid of "foreign" words, during which no one is killed, to massive murders of "unwanted" subgroups within a society, to wars with

Others. There are non-dangerous as well as genocidal purifications. For example, after Latvia gained its independence from the Soviet Union, its people wanted to get rid of some twenty "Russian" bodies in their national cemetery. Later in this book I will also describe another example: a genocidal purification following the collapse of the former Yugoslavia. Understanding the meaning and psychological necessity of purifications can help to develop strategies to keep shared prejudices within "normal" limits and prevent them from becoming destructive.

The signs of a *large-group progression* include forming stable families, clans, and professional subgroups; preserving individuality and having a large group in which individuals and professional organisations establish a capacity for compromise without damaging integrity (Rangell, 1980); and having an ability to question what is "moral" and "beautiful." A large group's basic trust returns. In a "healthy" large group there is an increased emphasis on freedom of speech; having just and functioning civil institutions, especially a fair legal system and mental hospitals with human care (Stern, 2001); and halting devaluation of women and children. Religion is culturally utilised for "togetherness" and loses its power to be a tool for magical thinking, bad prejudice, or political propaganda.

When a large group is *not* in a regressed state, its members (in general) can wonder about the enemy's *psychic reality*. To understand why the Other or its ancestors behaved in destructive ways does not mean forgiving and forgetting what happened before. It means performing the very difficult task of "humanising" the other large group. By studying the psychic reality of the enemy, new ways of dealing with the Other and its threat may emerge, instead of the attacked large group holding on to the enemy and the threat through maintaining its own regression.

CHAPTER SEVEN

Unending mourning and memorials

A corpse will not rise from its grave, but in order to deal with the fantasy that it might, people from different cultures put tombstones on graves or walls around graveyards. Mourning refers to the process of psychological burial of the mental double, the mental representation—a collection of images—of a dead person or lost thing. The physical burial of a corpse or the disappearance of a family home by fire does not remove the mental doubles of these lost entities from the mourner's mind. The mourner has to banish such representations to enclosures in the mind's far corners (through repression, denial, dissociation, displacement, and/or identification) so as not to be preoccupied with them. A "buried" mental representation however, unlike the physical one, is mobile. Some images can escape from their mental enclosure and continue to have an internal relationship with a mourner.

Freud's "Mourning and melancholia" (1917e) informs us about internal object relations. While sophisticated theories about such relations, such as those described by Kernberg (1976), would develop much later, Freud and many psychoanalysts who followed him, implied that an intense internal relation with images of the lost person or thing that constitutes the "normal" mourning process has a time limit: the mourning process ends when the mourner withdraws psychic investment in the representation of the lost object. Tähkä (1984) wrote that "normal" mourning only comes to a practical end when the image of the deceased or the lost thing becomes "futureless". We know that the re-activation of various images or the mental representation of the lost object in the mourner's mind can occur years after experiencing the loss, such as during the anniversary of a significant event that concerned the lost object before it was lost (anniversary reactions) (Pollock, 1989). Even so, the idea that "normal" mourning reaches an end has rarely been questioned. In truth, mourning never ends until the mourner dies; it only disappears for practical purposes when the mourner's relation- ship with the images of the lost person or thing no longer preoccupies the mourner's mind full force (Volkan & Zintl, 1993).

Before we examine the manifestations of mourning in large-group psychology, it will be helpful to take a look at individual mourning. Through the ever-increasing research on the infant mind, we now know that the infant is capable of performing many mental functions, includ- ing those that involve relating to others. We can picture these primitive functions as ego nuclei, as the evolution of sophisticated integration, coordination, and application of such ego functions requires some years. We cannot say that an infant and very small child are capable of maintaining a stable mental representation of the Other. Mourning, as studied by Freud and as described above, refers to an intense preoc- cupation with and the withdrawal from such preoccupation with the mental representation of the lost object. Losses that occur before the child is able to have and maintain stable mental representations result in the child's attempts to find substitute object relations and problems with attachment that may resemble the experience of feeling hunger. Edna Furman (1974) described long ago how small children cannot mourn as adults do.

As a child's mind develops, he experiences what can be called "developmental losses" as well as gains, such as giving up the mother's breasts and milk and achieving an ability to physically move away from and towards important objects at will. Children who slowly develop a lasting mental representation of the lost person, pet, or thing also slowly develop the concept of death and begin "learning" to mourn as an adult can. Even when they intellectually learn what death is on one level, belief in its reversibility remains, however hidden it may be, for some time.

Blos (1979) illustrated that regression during the adolescence passage "not only is unavoidable, it is obligatory, that is phase-specific" (p. 180). During this obligatory regression, the youngster revisits and reviews object relations with important others from childhood, family history, residuals of early traumas, and gender issues. This leads to the development of a lasting character structure. An adolescent modifies many existing childhood self—and object images and "gains" new identifications in order to crystallise a "new" self-representation and "new" object representations. Wolfenstein (1966) explained that going through the adolescence passage is a model for the true adult-type mourning process. In order to understand the impact of shared mourning in large-group psychology, the mourning concept I refer to in this chapter deals with the "adult type" of mourning.

In an adult, after a significant loss—a concrete one such as losing a person or an abstract one such as losing prestige—there is a grief reaction. The grief can be described as a mourner hitting his or her head against a wall while hoping that the wall will crack open and the lost object will rematerialise. After experiencing pain, when the wall does not crack open, the mourner experiences some kind of narcissistic hurt and anger—sometimes consciously but more often unconsciously. This verifies that a loss has taken place and the individual begins to "bury" its mental images. The mourner divides the mental representation of the lost object into hundreds of images and deals with them one by one, often repeatedly. If there are no complications, the mourner withdraws the mental investment from the lost person or thing's mental representation slowly, while identifying with some selected non-disturbing images and their functions that lead to a mental enrichment. A year or so after his father's death a philandering young man becomes a serious industrialist like his dead father used to be. A woman who depended on her husband to reinforce her sense of femininity may emerge from a healthy mourning feeling confident and womanly. An immigrant who had lost his country may create a symbolic representation of his country in a painting or song. Most identifications take place unconsciously. Such processes take months or years.

Those individuals who go through the developmental losses with great conflict, contaminating them with disturbing unconscious fantasies and experiencing a difficult adolescence passage will be less prepared to mourn as adults. The nature of the mental representation of the lost object in the mourner's mind, and conditions in which the loss has occurred, influence the mourning process. If the mental representation of the lost object was not only desired but "needed" for the mourner's maintenance of psychic stability or if the mourner had aggressive attachment to the object that was lost, mourning becomes complicated. If the loss occurs unexpectedly and drastically, such as through suicide or homicide, the aggression expressed in such events contaminates the necessary "normal" anger in grief and complicates the mourning process.

Freud (1917e) was aware of *unhealthy identifications*. If a mourner related to the lost person or thing with excessive ambivalence while this person still lived or the thing still existed, the mourner may end up identifying with the object representation of the lost item in "in toto" (Smith, 1975, p. 20). As Fenichel (1945) stated long ago, the mourner's "love" becomes the wish to keep this mental representation, and "hate" becomes the wish to hurt it. Since this ambivalently related mental representation is assimilated into the mourner's mind the mourner's self-representation turns into a battleground. Freud called this condition, "melancholia". When hate towards the assimilated mental representation of what has been lost becomes dominant, mourners may even attempt to kill themselves (suicide) in order to "kill" the assimilated object representation. In other words, they want to shoot, psychologically speaking, the object representation assimilated within their self-representation, and accordingly shoot themselves. Melancholia (depression) after a loss can be fatal for the mourner.

After a significant loss, some individuals do not go through "normal" mourning or do not develop depression; they become perennial mourners. Perennial mourners, to a large degree, cannot identify with the enriching aspects of the mental images of the lost object and adaptive ego functions associated with it. On the other hand, they do not end up identifying in a maladaptive way with the ambivalently related lost object representation. Instead, these mourners keep the object representation of the lost person or thing within their self-representation as a specific and unassimilated "foreign body" that excessively influences their self-representation. Such an unassimilated object representation or object image is known as an "introject". Although nowadays the term "introject" is seldom used in psychoanalytic writings, I suggest that we keep it, as it is most useful in explaining the internal world of a perennial mourner.

A man sought treatment in order to free himself from his younger brother's disturbing influence. He explained that while driving to work, his brother constantly talked with him, giving him advice about everything. He occasionally told his brother to shut up. Listening to him I imagined that he and his brother lived together in the same house or at least nearby, which would explain their riding together each workday to the downtown business area. Then he informed me that his younger brother had died in an accident six years earlier. The "brother" with whom he had conversations while driving to work was actually his brother's unassimilated object representation. Outside of conversing with his dead younger brother's object representation while driving to work, this man did not experience any break with reality.

Many perennial mourners are compulsive about reading obituary notices, making daily references to death, tombs, or graveyards, and talking about the dead in the present tense. Some of them "recognise" their lost ones in someone alive whom they encounter from a distance. The listener gets the impression that the speaker's daily life includes some actual current relationship with the deceased. If the lost item is a thing, the perennial mourner thinks about scenarios that involve finding and losing this object again and again. Such individuals also typically dream of the one who has died or the thing that is lost as still living or existing, but engaged in a life-and-death struggle. The dreamer then tries to rescue the person or thing—or to finish him, her, or it off. The outcome remains uncertain because the dreamer invariably awakens before the situation in the dream can be resolved. Often they use the term "frozen" when they speak of their dreams, reflecting their internal sense that they are stuck in their mourning process.

To have a "foreign body" within oneself is unpleasant. Therefore, most perennial mourners displace the unassimilated object image or representation of the lost person or thing onto "linking objects" or "linking phenomena" (Volkan, 1972, 1981; Volkan & Zintl, 1993). A linking object is a physical object, such as a special photograph of the deceased, a letter written by a soldier in the battlefield before being killed, or a gift the deceased made to the mourner before death; alternatively, it may be an animate object such as the dead person's pet. The object symbolises a meeting ground between the mental representation of a lost person or thing and the mourner's corresponding self-representation. Since it is "out there", the mourner's mourning process is externalised and symptoms described above are tamed. By controlling the linking objects or phenomena perennial mourners control their wish to "bring back" (love) or "kill" (hate) the lost object, and thus they avoid the psychological consequences of either of these two wishes.

Some individuals use linking phenomena such as a song or a repeating fantasy in order to perpetuate the possibility of contact between themselves and the lost person or thing. Linking objects and linking phenomena are not simple keepsakes. They are experienced by perennial mourners as "magical" and under their control. A keepsake does not function as a repository where a complicated mourning process is externalised. A typical keepsake provides continuity between the time before the loss and the time after the loss, or *generational continuity* if the lost person or item belonged to a previous generation. A typical picture of a dead father on a mantle is a keepsake. If a person puts this picture in a drawer and has an urgent desire to touch and examine it ritualistically, and a need to take it along in a suitcase when travelling, this picture is most likely being used as a linking object.

There are severely regressed adults, such as those with psychosis, who reactivate the transitional relatedness of their childhood and may recreate transitional objects or phenomena. A transitional object or phenomenon represents the first not-me experience, but it is never totally not-me. It links not-me with mother-me (Winnicott, 1953; Greenacre, 1969). Linking objects or phenomena should not be confused with childhood transitional objects and phenomena that are reactivated in adulthood. Linking objects or phenomena contain high-level symbolism. They must be thought of as tightly packed symbols whose significance is bound up in the conscious and unconscious nuances of the relationship that preceded the loss.

My further research on mourning (Volkan, 2007a, 2007b) led me to consider a blurring between "normal" unending mourning and perennial mourning when linking objects or phenomena become sources for positive behaviour patterns, reparative interpersonal relations, and even scientific inquiries. A linking object or phenomenon as a source of inspiration can give direction to creativity in some individuals. Complicated mourning still remains in these people, but now it is expressed in art forms. We would not refer to the person who created the Taj Mahal as pathological. My findings also remind me of Kernberg's (2010) description of "normal" unending mourning. He noted that a mourner has no possibility of correcting past shortcomings and failures in relation to the lost person or of obtaining that person's forgiveness. Thus, the mourner's reparative processes evolve as a "mandate", a "moral obligation", to act in accord with the wishes of the dead person.

Now I will turn my attention to large-group mourning. Observations of various types of transgenerational transmissions give us important clues about large-group mourning. The establishment of chosen traumas and entitlement ideologies are connected intimately with tens, hundreds, or millions of people who share unending mourning due to the same historic trauma. Members of the actually traumatised generation deposit their self-images linked to an inability to mourn into the next generation and give them the task of doing their parents' or grandparents' mourning. A similar process may continue to occur between future generations. A chosen trauma and an entitlement ideology reflect the existence of perennial mourning within the large group, whether it is actively experienced or whether it is hidden. Since I described these concepts earlier, here I will focus on another outcome of shared large-group mourning: building memorials.

Building memorial monuments or erecting other objects as memorials to remember lost persons or land after a trauma at the hands of enemies at first appears to be a cultural custom. Usually made out of marble or steel, memorial monuments are like boxes in which an affected group keeps their unfinished psychological processes locked up. A closer look at such memorials reveals that they may function as a *shared linking object* for a large group experiencing unending mourning (Volkan, 2007a). As architect Jeffrey Karl Ochsner (1997) states, "We choose to erect grave markers and monuments to commemorate the lives of the dead; we usually do not intend to build linking objects, although objects we do make clearly can serve us in this way" (p. 166). A memorial as a shared linking object is associated with the wish to complete a large group's mourning and help its members accept the reality of their losses. On the other hand, it is also associated with the wish to keep mourning active in the hope of recovering what was lost— this latter wish may fuel feelings of revenge. Both wishes can coexist: one wish can be dominant in relation to one memorial, while the other is dominant in relation to another memorial. Often a memorial monument as a shared linking object absorbs unfinished elements of incomplete mourning and helps the large group adjust to its current situation without re-experiencing the impact of the past losses, trauma, and their disturbing emotions (Volkan, 2006b).

The *Crying Father* memorial in Tskhinvali, the capital of South Ossetia, was built in the early 1990s to honor the memory of South Ossetians who were killed during the Georgia-South Ossetia War that occurred after Georgia regained its independence following the collapse of the Soviet Union. I will illustrate that the *Crying Father* memorial was used by South Ossetians not simply to keep the mourning process externalised, but also to fuel feelings of revenge.

My colleagues from the University of Virginia's Center for the Study of Mind and Human Interaction (CSMHI) and I first travelled to the Republic of Georgia and South Ossetia in the spring of 1998, and returned at least twice each year in the following four years. Our main purpose was to help the helpers of traumatised people; this region, with a population of approximately five million, contained more than 300,000 internally displaced people. For five years, CSMHI also facilitated a series of dialogues between Georgian and South Ossetian psychiatrists, psychologists, and other influential people, including those from the media and those from legal professions. This series of dialogues was designed to increase person-to-person interaction between Georgians and South Ossetians (Volkan, 2013). During our gatherings, the South Ossetian participants' references to the *Crying Father* memorial were clear indications of the intensity of their ongoing mourning process. They would speak about this memorial and subsequently change the subject whenever Georgian participants seemed to be ready to acknowledge their own side's role in the bloody conflict. The South Ossetians seemed unready to hear the Georgians' apology and empathy for South Ossetians' suffering.

When I first visited Tskhinvali, the *Crying Father* memorial had not yet been erected. I saw that the infrastructure of the city was basically ruined, and Tskhinvali School #5 on the city's Lenin Avenue, the future site of the *Crying Father* memorial, was no exception. Georgian forces had encircled Tskhinvali for many months during the Georgian-South Ossetian conflict, occupying many areas, including the city cemetery. Thus, when three young South Ossetian combatants died simultaneously during the 1991–1992 siege they were buried in the yard of School #5. The reasoning behind this decision was twofold: first, the school-yard was a safe place to bury them, and second, one of the victims had attended the school. In subsequent weeks, more and more dead defenders were buried there, including thirty who were apparently killed on the same day. Excepting a few people from a shelter for the elderly, no one who died of natural causes was buried there. Today there are about 100 graves in this schoolyard.

Grieving relatives built a chapel and later a statue, which they called the *Crying Father*, near the graves. The statue depicts a man dressed in a sheepskin hat and a *burka* (a traditional garment with long sleeves) looking down at the graves. In South Ossetian culture, men are not supposed to cry; the statue's paternal tears reflect extreme, ceaseless pain. An iron fence separates the cemetery from the rest of the schoolyard, but as one enters the yard, the statue is visible over the fence. From all three floors of the school, the schoolchildren—who began to attend the school after the hot conflict ended—can look out over the cemetery. Perhaps unsurprisingly, the schoolyard evolved into a sacred site, a symbol of South Ossetians' sense of victimisation by Georgian hands. The *Crying Father* memorial became a concrete symbol of continuing societal mourning.

During the initial years following the 1991–1992 conflict, there were repeated ceremonies in the yard of School #5. Using every possible excuse, authorities held them for various anniversaries and during religious holidays. The public supported the authorities by participating in such ceremonies en masse. Schoolchildren were encouraged to write and read poetry on victimisation, and, more importantly, on revenge. The image of the enemy was reinforced in order to maintain the group's illusion that it might recover its losses from its enemy. Most importantly, during each school day, hundreds of high school students would pass by the "sacred" site and, after the memorial was built, would see the "tears" of the *Crying Father*. The youngsters were constantly reminded of South Ossetia's victimisation, helplessness, and losses; they were exposed to these things in order to sustain their desire for revenge.

After several years of participation in CSMHI's Georgian-South Ossetian dialogue series, the South Ossetian participants acknowledged that the *Crying Father* monument was poisoning high school students and keeping negative feelings about Georgians alive in the younger generation. They spoke about this to the authorities in Tskhinvali, and later they reported that there were fewer ceremonies held in the yard of School #5. Also, the emotions in the poems read by the students were tamed. But the "poisoning" of youngsters passing by the *Crying Father* could not be changed. The South Ossetians participating in the dialogue series began to speak of their dilemma: they must either remove the graves to another location or build a new school. The first option was unthinkable because their religious beliefs forbade them to disturb the dead. On the other hand, the South Ossetian authorities, because of their extreme economic difficulties, could not afford to build a new school. When the South Ossetians began to verbalise their dilemma, they appeared more prepared to "hear" the Georgians' apology. When a Georgian said that she was moved by the South Ossetians' dilemma and that she wanted to go to School #5 to pay her respects to the dead, the South Ossetians responded to her positively.

There are other memorials that also evolved as shared linking objects, but which were associated with functions unlike those of the *Crying Father*, such as Yad Vashem in Jerusalem. Visiting it definitely induces strong feelings in Israelis, and indeed in all those who allow themselves to feel the impact of the Holocaust. Yad Vashem is a shared linking object that keeps the group's mourning alive. Since the losses incurred during the Holocaust are too vast to be mourned, a monument like Yad Vashem functions as a place where mourning is felt and, in a sense, "stored". Since there have been countless ways to recall and express feelings of mourning regarding the Holocaust—in religious or political ceremonies, in books, in poems, in art, in movies, in conferences— Yad Vashem is not associated with keeping the wounds caused by the Holocaust alive in the hope of recovering what has been lost; it is not associated with a deep sense of revenge. On the other hand, the task of mourning the Holocaust is passing from generation to generation (for the relevant literature, see Volkan, Ast & Greer, 2002), and the monument links the descendants to their lost ancestors. It keeps the mourning alive without major or observable revengeful consequences.

In the United States, the Vietnam Veterans Memorial also evolved as a shared linking object (K. Volkan, 1992; Ochsner, 1997) and helped Americans to accept that their losses were real and that life would go on without recovering them. While there were many massive protests against the war in Vietnam, I do not think that, in general, Americans felt themselves to be the guilty party. Communism was "bad", and the American war in Vietnam was for the "good" of humankind. This was the "official" view and the Vietnam War did not make the Americans feel as if they were the "bad" guys. But, certainly, many felt that dying for causes in a faraway land was not justified. Thus, the Vietnam War divided American society. When the war came to an end, "the most common response was, in effect, denial" (Ochsner, 1997, p. 159). The dead were mourned by family members and friends and were buried quietly. "However, the construction of the Vietnam Veterans Memorial, with the inscribed names of the dead and missing, seemed to change all this" (p. 159). The memorial's young designer, Maya Ying Lin, while planning her design, associated death with "a sharp pain that lessens with time, but can never quite heal over a scar" (Campbell, 1983, p. 150). She wanted to take a knife and cut open the earth, and "with time the grass would heal it" (p. 150). Kurt Volkan (1992) looked at the Vietnam Veterans Memorial from a psychological angle and showed how this memorial became a shared linking object wherein the images of the dead were linked with the corresponding images of the mourners. "By touching the stone and the etching of the names, the living bonded with the dead—after all, a name is a symbolic term that embodies everything about one's existence" (p. 76). He added: "Thus, this Wall [the monument] can be as personal as a mother crying for her lost son, or as public as a nation weeping for a past history that has yet to be resolved" (p. 76).

The Vietnam Veterans Memorial not only opened a wound, but also helped Americans to develop scars to cover the wound. When a monument becomes a shared linking object that is associated with this type of function by the public, it may function in the long run as a "locked box" (Volkan, 1988, p. 171) that contains the group's unresolved shared emotions. This is what has happened in the case of the Vietnam Veterans Memorial. Kurt Volkan (1992) wrote: "The Vietnam War memorial has created a permanent link between the living and the dead. By 'burying' 57,692 of our soldiers in one place, we are instantly connected to the land and the surrounding area, and we are constantly reminded of the past. It is one of the many ways of claiming this land as our own, as a 'linking object' that will tie the living to the dead forever" (p. 77).

Many memorial monuments are works of art. But sometimes appreciation of them as art forms takes time; they have to stop being "hot" (emotionally speaking) before their beauty can be appreciated. Some monuments also have a "change function" according to what goes on within the large group whose members and their descendants have been affected by the shared massive trauma. New hostilities with the old or new enemy can make such monuments "hot" again. Otherwise, years or even centuries can pass before previously "hot" places cool off, and we remember them periodically during anniversaries of events surrounding them.

Later, in Chapter Nine, I will examine the psychology of the Kosovo memorial in the service of reopening acute mourning and creating time collapse.

CHAPTER EIGHT

Political leaders' personalities

The personalities of our political leaders, in a general sense but not necessarily a psychoanalytic one, have always been scrutinised, especially during elections, crises, or scandals. There is public interest in understanding a political leader's personality and its role in determining the leader's behaviour and decision making. Over the course of a lifetime, an adult exhibits habitual behaviour and thought patterns that can be observed by others. Because political leaders spend a great deal of time in the public eye and have little choice but to allow their modes of speech, bodily gestures, emotional expressions, and other personal habitual patterns to be viewed by anyone with access to the media, attempts are sometimes made to analyse their personality, mostly by persons who have not even studied human psychology.

The term "personality" describes the observable and predicable repetitions that individuals consciously and unconsciously utilise under ordinary circumstances to maintain a stable reciprocal relationship between themselves and their environment. Therefore, personality is associated with self-regulatory and environment-altering ego functions that individuals use regularly to maintain both internal (intrapsychic) and interpersonal harmony. Two additional concepts, *temperament* and *character*, are usually included under the umbrella of personality.

Temperament refers to genetically and constitutionally determined cognitive and affectomotor tendencies. Character is formed by the ego-syntonic modes individuals utilise to reconcile intrapsychic conflicts during developmental years. When temperament and character are combined, they produce adult personality.

The concept of personality, however, is not the same as identity—the latter is not observed by others, but instead is sensed only by a specific individual. The term personality should also be differentiated from "self-representation", another term that refers to a psychoanalyst's metapsychological description of how a patient's self-organisation (or *personality organisation*) has developed, and how it theoretically relates to object representations as well as id demands, ego functions, and superego influences.

In our clinical work we observe various types of personalities and name them: *obsessive, paranoid, phobic, depressive, narcissistic*, and so on. For example, when we see a patient who is habitually dogmatic, opinionated, ambivalent and "clean", and who exhibits stiff and rigid gestures, and cannot freely express emotions, we say that this patient has an *obsessive personality*. Most people, however, possess aspects of different personality characteristics and it is difficult to classify their predictable behaviour, thought, and emotional patterns as strictly one type or another. When such patterns are exaggerated, maladaptive, predictable, and cause interpersonal problems, mental health professionals use terms such as "personality disorder". For example, a "routine" obsessional personality evolves into a "disorder" when patients exhibit ambivalence to such a degree that they constantly frustrate others or cannot complete their own tasks. People with obsessive personality disorder also keep their emotions under control, but on occasion lose control in aggressive and inappropriate outbursts that cause further interpersonal conflicts. They are like a chronically constipated person who suddenly has an explosive bowel movement. I use this anal analogy because, through clinical work dating back to Freud (1905d) and Abraham (1921), we have become aware of the anal fixations of the obsessional personality. Often, however, individuals do not recognise their own part in causing interpersonal problems, or the role of their own personality in such conflicts.

The personality of political leaders plays a crucial role in their attempts to maintain a stable relationship both with those who are in their immediate "entourage" and with the much larger group of people who comprise their "followers". The leader–follower relationship is a "two-way" street: it is influenced and determined by the leader's personality, and by the followers' shared conscious and unconscious wishes and needs. A political leader may utilise the historical arena to find external solutions for internal, mostly unconscious, needs, wishes and conflicts, and in that case it is the leader's needs, wishes and conflicts that will modify the emotional and physical state of the followers.

Political science professor James MacGregor Burns (1984) identified two types of leaders: *transactional* and *transforming*. The transactional leader depends on, and in fact thrives on, bargaining, manipulating, accommodating, and compromising within a given system. He or she acts according to political polls and national "climate" and follows existing large-group sentiments, becoming a spokesperson for them. In contrast, a transforming leader "responds to fundamental human needs and wants, hopes and expectations" and may "transcend and even seek to reconstruct the political system, rather than simply operating within it" (Burns, 1984, p. 16). In this we hear an echo of Weber's (1923) classic description of charismatic leaders. As charismatic leaders they can be reparative, destructive, or both (Volkan, 2006a). They are reparative if they attempt to uplift their followers to higher levels without malignant propaganda against, or deliberate destruction of, those considered the Other. On the other hand, some transforming leaders try to destroy the Other in order to raise the status of their large group.

Nelson Mandela's reparative approach to leading post-apartheid South Africa is evident in his involvement in the 1995 Rugby World Cup hosted by South Africa. Rugby had been considered a white man's sport in South Africa and "a symbol of white Afrikaner unity and pride dating back to the Boer War" (Swift, 1995, p. 32), and although South Africa had produced talented rugby teams, they had been banned from the first two Rugby World Cups in 1987 and 1991 because of apartheid. Hosting the 1995 World Cup was therefore of great political significance for the new South Africa, and Mandela could enhance both national and international prestige if the event was successful.

Mandela's task was made even more challenging since the South African team, the Springboks, had only one black player, and the team's name itself invoked associations with apartheid. But instead of simply ensuring a well-run tournament and portraying South Africa as a reformed and responsible host, Mandela's personality actually helped to promote the process of emotional unification in South

Africa. To encourage the feeling that rugby now belonged to all South Africans, he visited the team's training camp, shook hands with the players, patted their backs, and wore a Springbok cap. He told the team that the whole nation was behind them and began to make public statements about the Springboks' new image. The Springboks reciprocated. The day before their match against the former champion, Australia, the South African rugby team went to Robben Island, off Cape Town, where Mandela had been imprisoned for eighteen years. They visited Mandela's former cell and dedicated their efforts in the World Cup to their president. The whole country was galvanised. The next day, under the spell of this emotional atmosphere, the Springboks defeated Australia 27–18.

On the day before the Springbok's next match against France, Mandela gave a speech in Ezakheni, a black community, where he pointed to his Springbok cap and said, "This cap does honor to our boys. I ask you to stand by them tomorrow because they are our kind" (Swift, 1995, p. 32). South African blacks identified with Mandela and with his acceptance of the white regime's sport, and the unlikely symbol of South Africa's apartheid past was transformed into a symbol of unity and hope for the modification of societal attitudes. Millions cheered the team's upset of France the next day, and the 1995 Rugby World Cup came to a crescendo when South Africa defeated top-ranked New Zealand in overtime to win the championship. Soon afterwards, the Springboks began a campaign to encourage black township residents to pay their utility bills as part of their contribution to the rebuilding of South Africa. A white man's sport had become a vehicle for education about civil responsibility, adaptation, and post-apartheid politics.

Let us compare Nelson Mandela with Slobodan Milošević. Both were transforming leaders, and they responded to the crisis of systemic dissolution, large-group regression, and questions about large-group identity in very different ways. Mandela's substantive as well as symbolic actions have collectively "taught" South Africans, both black and white, how to usefully adapt to new social and political challenges, and the emotional legacy of apartheid. Milošević, following the collapse of the former Yugoslavia, successfully ignited virulent Serbian nationalism and helped Serbs come together as a cohesive group through their shared sense of victimisation, and their demonisation of and desire for revenge against an enemy symbolised by Yugoslav Muslims.

After the collapse of Yugoslavia, when Serbs were attempting to consolidate their "new" identity, Milošević encouraged them to adopt political doctrines of entitlement and purification rather than cooperation and coexistence. It would be misleading to portray Milošević as solely responsible for the many tragedies of the Balkans, since animosity between Croats, Serbs, and Bosniaks existed long before he came to power, and many complex issues and events were involved. There was traffic from both sides of a two-way street. But it is also clear that the decisions Milošević made were not intended to encourage peace, stability, and ethnic tolerance.

I have not studied in depth the development of Nelson Mandela's personality and therefore cannot offer many insights into how or why he became the type of leader that he did, or why he made certain decisions. I did, however, gather detailed information on Slobodan Milošević's inner life and personality (Volkan, 1997, 2006a). In the next chapter I will tell the story of Milošević and his involvement in destructive large-group processes.

In a stable democracy that is not experiencing economic, military, and political stress, the personality of a transactional leader is not usually of critical importance, and even a transforming leader will not cause fundamental changes in society or initiate drastically different policies. The formal and informal systems of "checks and balances" in a well-functioning democracy prevent a leader's habitual ways of behaving and feeling from exerting undue influence over government and the governed. Even when many followers are excited about and identify with a transforming leader's personality, behaviour, and agenda, changes that may result are not typically drastic.

It is true that the development of civilisation appears to be different from large group to large group. Such differences are a matter of degree, however, since highly civilised large groups can also regress. This is why technological advances should not be considered a good measuring stick for judging the progress of civilisation. Under circumstances such as political or economic crises, revolution, terrorism, war-like situations, or war however, the personality of a political leader can and usually will influence outcomes or policies. At times it can even be a major factor in creating new and drastic societal and political processes. Leaders also experience sustained anxiety or unpleasant emotions such as depression or humiliation due to the reactivation of their internal mental conflicts (whatever their cause), and they may utilise the societal or political arena in an attempt to find an external solution for an internal dilemma. At such times a leader's personality plays a key role in the "choice" of which societal or political process a large group initiates or becomes involved in.

An individual's established personality tells us a great deal about how he or she will respond to regression and anxiety-producing situations. For example, because obsessional individuals have difficulty tolerating loss of control, we would expect a leader with such a personality to experience internal danger and anxiety if faced with a political situation or a political rival that cannot be controlled. The person may then unconsciously experience loss of love or self-esteem. The obsessional leader may respond in an exaggerated fashion and seek rules, regulations, and official policies or other sources of rationalisation and intellectualisation to address the crisis at the expense of exploring creative and adaptive solutions. Or he or she may exhibit extreme ambivalence toward the "uncontrolled" opponent and behave in irrational ways.

There are also other types of leaders, such as paranoid ones. For example, recalling Joseph Stalin, Nikita Khrushchev (1970) wrote: "It's one thing not to trust people. That was his [Stalin's] right, even though his extreme mistrust did indicate that he had a serious psychological problem. But it's another thing when a man is compulsively driven to eliminate *anyone* he doesn't trust" (p. 307). See also Tucker's (1973) detailed biography of Stalin as a pathologically paranoid leader. It is often difficult to differentiate a paranoid style, which may help a leader to protect the large group from what will slowly, inescapably, grow into the pathologically paranoid leader.

In 1926(d) Freud proposed four situations that are internally dangerous and induce anxiety in an individual. The first is the fear of the loss of a love object. The second involves fear of losing the love provided by the love object. The third can be described as losing a body part and is associated with fear of castration. The fourth danger refers to the fear of not living up to the internalised expectations of important others (superego) and therefore reflects a loss of self-esteem. When an external situation is unconsciously perceived as echoing one of these threats, or a combination of them, their images become part of internal mental conflicts and the individual may experience anxiety and regress. Freud's remarks are basically applicable to patients with neurotic personality organisation, persons with integrated self-representation. At the present time psychoanalysts are treating many individuals with narcissistic and borderline personality organisations, persons with unintegrated self-representation. Also, we know that many individuals with narcissistic personality organisation search out leadership roles (Volkan, 2004; Volkan & Fowler, 2009). Therefore, I wish to expand Freud's list and describe more internal situations that cause anxiety for persons, including leaders, who posses narcissistic personality organisation.

Narcissism is linked to self-preservation and in human functioning it is as normal as sex, aggression, and anxiety (Rangell, 1980). As such, it is subject to variations. It can be "healthy", or "unhealthy". A child with a healthy narcissism, in growing independent, loves himself not only when feeling loved by the members of the family, but also when rejected by others (Weigert, 1967). As an adult this person is capable of maintaining self-esteem when facing losses or traumas. In American psychoanalytic circles in the 1960s and 1970s a concentrated effort was made, especially by Kohut and Kernberg, to study individuals with unhealthy, exaggerated narcissism. Kohut posited an independent line of development from autoerotism through narcissism that is adaptive and culturally valuable. Maternal shortcomings lead to a fixation in the child and the child develops a grandiose and exhibitionistic self-image that Kohut called the "grandiose self". If the maternal shortcomings have not been too great, the grandiose self is transformed into a self with mature ambitions and self-esteem (Kohut, 1966, 1971, 1977). While Kohut was developing his metapsychological understanding of narcissism following Jacobson (1964), Kernberg focused on object relations conflict when he described persons who have narcissistic personality organisation. In such individuals, he illustrated, the libidinal investment is not directed toward a normally integrated self-structure; such individuals possess an unintegrated self-structure and exhibit object relations conflicts (Kernberg, 1975–1976, 1980).

As I described earlier, an infant is fed four to six times a day. Each feeding experience produces different degrees of pleasure (Stern, 1985). As the child grows up, in a sense, different experiences become categorised in the child's mind as "good" and "bad". Loving and frustrating, as well as loved and frustrated, aspects of people connected with these experiences are divided too until the integrative function is effectively accomplished. As I described in Chapter Two, the child's *subjective sense* of integrated self is the child's personal identity. If the child cannot fully accomplish the integrative task, due to biological as well as environmental reasons, the individual's identity, even in adulthood, remains divided. For persons like those with narcissistic personality organisation, the normal *developmental splitting* evolves as a *defensive splitting*. In other words, as they grow up, such individuals continue to maintain two unintegrated parts.

Object relations conflict refers to tensions concerning integrating or not integrating libidinally and aggressively loaded self—and object images within, or externalising them on to others and re-internalising them. Kernberg also used the term "grandiose self" in describing the libidinally loaded omnipotent part of the self that such patients usually exhibit overtly. The second and usually hidden part of individuals with narcissistic personality organisation that is associated with dependency and inferiority is called their "hungry self" (Volkan, 2010). These two parts are separated by a defensive splitting mechanism.

There are various types of adjustment to narcissistic personality organisation. For example, there are even individuals with masochistic narcissistic personality organisation who hide their grandiose selves behind a behaviour pattern that says, "I am the number one sufferer in the world" (Cooper, 1989; Volkan, 2010). Those who can hold on to their grandiose selves daily by finding a fit between its demands and the environment, as well as those people who can establish sublimations, or even sometimes those who have what Kernberg (1975) called "pseudo-sublimations", can effectively hide their utilisation of defensive splitting. They make "successful" adjustments to life. By "successful" I am not only referring to the individual's standing in society. I am also describing the stability of the grandiose self and its verification by others so that a fit occurs between the individual's internal demand and his interpersonal relationships. Others consider such a person who usually emerges as a leader of an organisation or even a country, to be someone who *is* superior. But when persons with narcissistic personality organisation face threats against their grandiose parts, they experience anxiety.

Leaders who have narcissistic personalities are preoccupied with self-importance and fantasies of unbounded success to which they feel entitled. While they demand admiration from others, they are aloof and without empathy towards them. They are compelled to be "number one" in power, prestige and fame, and split off and deny their "hungry", dependent and devalued aspects. Such a person may be deeply involved with politics and social issues, but regards them unilaterally without reference to the views of others who are perceived as "inferior", and remains essentially indifferent to and "above" humanity in general. Although the narcissistic leader may appear aloof, and therefore indicate the possibility of an obsessional character, obsessional individuals are emotionally far more in tune with those around them, and are often capable of sincere and passionate concern for social and political issues (Kernberg, 1970).

Another characteristic of some people with a narcissistic personality is their conscious or unconscious fantasy that they live by themselves in a splendid, but lonely "kingdom" under a "glass bubble" (Volkan, 1979b). Through the metaphorical glass they watch others outside their "kingdom" and divide them into two groups: those who support their narcissism and those who are devalued. Those devalued may be perceived as an "enemy", or may be disregarded as completely insignificant. When a narcissistic leader's superiority and power are threatened, he or she experiences shame and humiliation. Feelings of rage may follow. In order to stabilise or re-establish grandiosity and remove discomforting feelings, the leader is then internally compelled to act, and the decisions that result may have drastic societal or political consequences.

A study of the thirty-seventh US President Richard Nixon's adult life reveals that he had a successful narcissistic personality organisation and also utilised obsessional mechanisms to support his narcissism (Volkan, Itzkowitz & Dod, 1997). He was preoccupied with power and superiority and being "number one"—first with achieving it and later with defending it from the many "enemies" he perceived around him. According to his wife, since the time they met in college, Nixon had always been "president of some group like the 20–30 Club, and this, that and the other thing" (Mazo & Hess, 1967, p. 30). He ran in thirteen elections, starting with class president in high school, and only lost three. At the age of thirty-three he was elected to the US Congress, became a US Senator at the age of thirty-seven, and at the age of thirty-nine became the second youngest US Vice President. As president, he continued to collect important or "historic" achievements that included being the first US president to visit China, as well as many lesser and even seemingly trivial "firsts" that he instructed those in his entourage to record for posterity. According to his aide John Ehrlichman, "There was a running gag on any campaign; everything that happened was a 'historic first'" (Volkan, Itzkowitz & Dod, 1997, p. 94).

Like other persons with "glass bubble" fantasies, Nixon was a loner who seemed to arrive at many decisions by talking to himself in private. He did have close advisers, and certainly worked closely with and respected the opinions of his Secretary of State, Henry Kissinger, yet he was not a patient listener. According to Roger Ailes, one of his aides in the White House, "He knew what you were going to talk about. He generally knew what your opinion was, already knew what his answer would be" (Volkan, Itzkowitz & Dod, 1997, p. 99). But in spite of, or even perhaps because of this narcissistic personality, Nixon was a highly successful politician and at times an effective and respected president.

However, there are several examples of periods when Nixon responded to "shame and humiliation" and made decisions to re-establish his narcissistic personality that had widespread and devastating repercussions. Steinberg (1996), a political scientist as well as a psychoanalyst, notes that the frustration and humiliation that Nixon encountered in dealing with the war in Vietnam at the outset of his first administration, as well as a series of unrelated events, prompted Nixon to lash out and seek a target through which he could address the needs of his narcissistic personality and restore his power and prestige in his own mind.

Part of Nixon's election campaign of 1968 was to end the Vietnam War "with honor", yet the North Vietnamese would not come to the bargaining table on terms acceptable to Nixon, launched a new offensive into South Vietnam, fired rockets into Saigon, and were perceived as otherwise trying to test, thwart, and humiliate him. Domestic sources also added to Nixon's humiliation. Within the first year of his administration, two of his Supreme Court nominations were rejected by the Senate, the threat of anti-war student demonstrations prevented him from attending his daughter Julie's graduation from Smith College and his son-in-law David's from Amherst, and the Apollo 13 moon mission was aborted, leaving Nixon "frustrated, angry and embarrassed" (Steinberg, 1996, p. 185). The shame and humiliation brought on by this series of events induced internal danger signals.

I will now examine the idea that to re-establish the stability of his narcissistic personality organisation in the face of these threats, Nixon hastily chose to exert and reconfirm his power and superiority through a *secret* offensive against North Vietnamese and Viet Cong sanctuaries in Cambodia. There is strong evidence that Nixon reached the decision to bomb Cambodia while he was in his "lonely kingdom" under a "glass bubble" in an airplane flying from Washington, D.C. to Brussels, and that his decision was made without consulting the relevant advisers, "in the absence of a detailed plan" (Kissinger, 1979, p. 242). The plane ride was the beginning of Nixon's ten-day ceremonial visit to Europe, which of course had been planned much earlier. The day before the flight, on 22 February 1969, the North Vietnamese had renewed their offensive actions. One can easily imagine, from a *realpolitik* point of view, that Nixon's decision to bomb was a response to the renewed North Vietnamese offensive. At that time, Cambodia, a monarchy with seven million subjects, was trying to stay neutral, even though the North Vietnamese had established sanctuaries in the border area between the two countries. Earlier, Nixon had examined research and intelligence that indicated that bombing these sanctuaries would drive the North Vietnamese further west and deeper into Cambodia, perhaps eventually causing Cambodia to fall to the communist regime, and so he had decided not to attack the bases (Hersh, 1983). Why did he change his mind suddenly without any consultation? I suggest that there were factors emanating from his narcissistic personality organisation. Later he would state how he took the North Vietnamese move as a personal attack. He wrote that this move "was a test, clearly designed to take the measure of me and my administration at the outset. My immediate instinct was to retaliate" (Nixon, 1978, p. 380).

Upon Kissinger's request, Nixon agreed to postpone his decision for forty-eight hours, then later cancelled the original bombing plan. He ordered another strike on 9 March, only to rescind it a second time. The first B-52 raid on North Vietnamese bases in Cambodia finally commenced on the morning of 18 March, but was kept secret from the American public. Kissinger was told to inform the State Department of the first B-52 mission "only after the point of no return ... the order is not appealable" (Ambrose, 1989, p. 258). Only after ordering the retaliation on North Vietnamese bases in Cambodia did Nixon meet with some of his advisers, giving them the impression that their input would be considered even though the first attack was *fait accompli*. The second attack took place in mid-April, and Cambodia was invaded on 1 May 1970.

What interest me are the code names of the Cambodia bombings: The first one was "Breakfast" and the second was "Lunch". "Lunch"," according to Kissinger, was based in part on another humiliating situation. This time, the desire was to retaliate against North Korea, which had recently shot down a US spy plane: "But as always when suppressing his instinct for a jugular response, Nixon looked for some other place to demonstrate his mettle. There was nothing he feared more than to be thought weak" (Kissinger, 1979, p. 247). I have no idea who came up with the code names pertaining to food. I will speculate that "Breakfast" and "Lunch" might be for Nixon's "hungry self"! If his "hungry self" was fed, then his "grandiose self" would not be threatened. We also know that "Lunch" was succeeded by the code name "Dinner", and then eventually expanded into the entire "Menu".

There was more to the decision to bomb Vietnamese sanctuaries in Cambodia—made quickly, secretively, and exclusively by Nixon—and later invading Cambodia than military strategy. The North Vietnamese would not be allowed to get away with making Nixon appear weak, impotent, or indecisive. In the public speech in which Nixon announced his invasion of Cambodia, delivered nearly a year after the covert bombing began, the importance of the policy as a means of supporting a sense of grandiosity (now displaced on the US) seems clear. He said, "We will not be humiliated ... we will not be defeated." Under no circumstance would the United States act "like a pitiful, helpless giant"—instead America must respond decisively since "it is not our power but our will and character that is being tested tonight" (Ambrose, 1989, p. 345).

Student protests broke out across the nation, and nearly 100,000 protesters eventually converged on Washington. The bombing of Cambodia marked the beginning of a fully fledged civil war that raged for five years. After it ended, between 1975 and 1979, an estimated 1.7 million people were killed and buried in "Killing Fields" as the Khmer Rouge sought complete control over Cambodia.

In the next chapter I will return to Slobodan Milošević and illustrate a reactivation of a chosen trauma with very deadly consequences.

CHAPTER NINE

Reactivation of a chosen trauma

This chapter describes the reactivation of Serbs' chosen trauma in 1989, the shared mental double of the Battle of Kosovo of 1389, and its consequences. When typical historical and political accounts were written after this event took place there were usually no references to the individual and large-group psychology that took central stage in this human drama. By providing certain details, I want to illustrate how utilising psychoanalytic insights about individual and large-group psychology in their own right expand our knowledge of history. I also wish to illustrate that if psychological insights had been available to international decision makers with power at the time this chosen trauma was reactivated, strategies might have been developed to prevent deadly outcomes.

I will start with a brief story of the Battle of Kosovo. After becoming independent from Byzantium in the twelfth century, the kingdom of Serbia thrived for almost 200 years under the leadership of the Nemanjić dynasty, reaching its climax under the beloved Emperor Stefan Dušan. By the end of his twenty-four-year reign, Serbia covered a territory from the Croatian border in the north to the Aegean Sea in the south, from the Adriatic Sea in the west to Constantinople (present-day Istanbul) in the east. Dušan died in 1355 and the Nemanjić dynasty came to an end a short time thereafter. In 1371, Serbian feudal lords elected Lazar Hrebeljanović as leader of Serbia, though he assumed the title of Prince or Duke rather than King or Emperor. The decline of Serbia that followed is primarily attributed to the expansion of the Ottoman Empire into Serbian territory, culminating in the Battle of Kosovo on 28 June 1389 at the Kosovo Polje (the Field of the Black Birds) in the southern part of the Yugoslav Federation. Despite a gap of some seventy years between the Battle of Kosovo and the total occupation of Serbia by the Ottoman Turks, a belief gradually developed that equated the two events.

There are many versions of the "historical truth" of the Battle of Kosovo (Emmert, 1990). We know that the Ottoman Sultan, Murad I, was fatally wounded by a Serbian assassin during or after the battle. We also know that the wounded Sultan or his son Bayezid ordered the execution of Prince Lazar, who had been captured during the battle. Chroniclers have disagreed, however, on other outcomes of the battle. With heavy losses on both sides and the deaths of both leaders, many consider the immediate result of the battle to be indecisive. Ottoman forces apparently returned to Adrianople (Edirne) after Kosovo, and Lazar was succeeded by his son, Stefan Lazarević, who later became an ally of Murad's successor.

Seventy years later, however, the Ottomans had gained substantial control over Serbia, and the Battle of Kosovo slowly began to evolve into a "chosen trauma" for the Serbian people. Mythologised tales of the battle were transmitted from generation to generation through a strong oral and religious tradition in Serbia, perpetuating and reinforcing Serbians' chosen trauma. What is important in this case is not only the historical truth, but the impact of the shared mental representation of the "chosen trauma" on a large group's identity. Markovic (1983) refers to the memory of Kosovo as a "sacred grief" (p. 111) and adds that "mere mention of that name suffices to shake a Serb to the depths of his soul" (p. 111).

There is ample evidence to support the fact that the "interpretation" of events at the Battle of Kosovo has gone through various transformations. For example, early chronicles of the Battle of Kosovo did not specify the name of Sultan Murad's assassin. One version of the story says that a small group of Lazar's soldiers slipped through Ottoman defences and one was able to stab Murad, another says Lazar himself led this group, while a 1497 account identifies Miloš Kobila (or Kobilić or Obravitch), one of Lazar's son-in-laws who had been accused of being a traitor prior to the battle, as the heroic assassin. After some time, Miloš was accepted as the actual assassin.

As the "chosen trauma" evolved, several factors, including the disunity of the Balkan Slavs and even that of Lazar's own family, Lazar's apparent ineffectiveness as a leader, and the continued existence of Serbia for many decades after the battle, were "repressed." As a shared "object representation" involved in transgenerational transmission of the Serbians' traumatised self-representations, Lazar initially had to be absolved for sealing the fate of Serbia. According to legend, Saint Ilya, in the shape of a gray falcon, appeared before Lazar on the eve of the battle with a message from the Virgin Mary. Lazar was given two choices: 1) if he wished, he could win the battle and find a kingdom on earth or 2) he could lose the battle, die a martyr's death, and find a kingdom in heaven. The following is a version of a Serbian folk song about Lazar's dilemma:

> Dear God, what shall I do and
> Which kingdom should I choose?
> Should I choose the Kingdom of Heaven
> Or the kingdom of Earth?
> If I choose the kingdom,
> The kingdom of the Earth,
> The earthly kingdom is of short duration
> And the Heavenly is from now to eternity.
> (From Markovic, 1983, p. 114)

The legend says that, being a devoutly religious person, Lazar "chose" defeat and death. Through the proliferation of this legend the Serbians collectively tried to deny shame and humiliation. But helplessness and victimisation could not be denied since the Serbians, under Ottoman control, had no power to bring back their glorious past. They held on to the "martyrdom" of the legend and identified their large-group identity with it. In fact, the sense of martyrdom fit well with their pre-Ottoman perception of themselves. Even during the Nemanjić period, the Serbians thought that they had sacrificed themselves for other Christians in Europe as they had served as a "buffer" against the advancing Muslim Turks. The Serbians, belonging to the Greek

Orthodox Church, however, received no appreciation from their Roman Catholic neighbours in Europe for their "sacrifice".

As a result of these traumatised and transmitted self-representations pertaining to the same "chosen trauma", the Serbians held on to an identity of victimhood and became, as a large group, "perennial mourners" of the loss at Kosovo. Of course, the reality that they were occupied by the Ottomans supported this shared perception, and the Church and folksingers effectively kept the "chosen trauma" in the public eye. June 28, the day of the Battle of Kosovo, was commemorated as St. Vitus Day and through the centuries became the subject of other legends that strengthened the victimised large-group identity.

The Field of Black Birds remained a symbol of unending mourning and helplessness which could not be reversed by the Serbians living under Ottoman rule. A folk story sprang up saying that the flowers on the mountainous plain of the Kosovo battlefield were "crying"— referring to their bent stems upon which blossoms appeared like heads bowed in grief.

The Ottomans did not directly force the Serbians to convert to Islam— except for the youngsters they collected to go through the *devşirme* system. Briefly, *devşirme* involved conscripting state servants from the Ottoman Empire's Christian orthodox population. It started with the reign of Murad I who was also killed during the Battle of Kosovo in 1359 and continued for the next four centuries. Christian orthodox youth, such as Serbian youngsters, were collected as an extraordinary tax levied by the Sultan, taken from their families, converted to Islam, and educated to serve the Sultan. One of the greatest grand viziers of the Ottoman Empire, Sokollu (Sokolovich) Mehmed Pasha, for example, was originally a Serb who had risen within the *devşirme* system. Most Serbian (and other former Christian) youngsters, however, would be enrolled in the ranks of the military as members of the empire's feared Janissary force.

After the Ottomans moved into Balkan territory, "The Orthodox Patriarch himself testified in a letter to the Pope in 1385 that the Sultan left to his church complete liberty of action" (Kinross, 1965, p. 59). Even during the reign of Murad I, the seeds of the multicultural, multireligious, and multilingual society of the Ottoman Empire had been sown. Nevertheless, "in the Ottoman Empire everyone was equal, but the Muslims were more equal" (Volkan & Itzkowitz, 1994, p. 64). Thus, some Slavs gradually became Muslims during the first two centuries of Ottoman rule, especially in Bosnia, a greay area between Orthodox and Roman Catholic influence. During the Ottoman period these ancestors of today's Bosnian Muslims became the middle—and upper-middle-class city dwellers in Bosnia-Herzegovina, while peasants in Serbia and Croatia remained Orthodox and Roman Catholic. By the middle of the sixteenth century, half of the population of Bosnia was Muslim, and Sarajevo was nearly all Muslim.

Among those who remained Christian, the idea that Prince Lazar, and by extension the Serbians, had chosen a Kingdom in Heaven rather than a kingdom on earth remained alive in a rather covert fashion—except during some rebellions such as the one in 1804–1815. The Serbs held on to their victimised identity and glorified victimisation in songs such as the following:

> Drink, Serbs, of God's glory
> And fulfill the Christian law;
> And even though we have lost our kingdom,
> Let us not lose our souls. (Markovic, 1983, p. 116)

In the latter part of the nineteenth century, however, as the decline of the Ottoman Empire coincided with the awakening of nationalism in Europe, other aspects of the Lazar and Kosovo legends became more readily observable. Lazar was first transformed from an ineffective leader to a saint and martyr, but slowly Lazar's and Miloš's images were changed from martyr, victim, and tragic figure to hero and then ultimately to avenger. For example, while paintings and icons of Lazar and Miloš from the Renaissance typically depicted them as saintly or Christ-like, some from the late nineteenth and early twentieth centuries featured them as increasingly strong and warrior-like figures. There would be no shared Serbian identity outside the context of the symbol of Kosovo, whether it induced a shared sense of victimisation or a shared sense of revenge. Mothers began to greet their children as the "avengers of Kosovo"—the direct and indirect message was to reverse not only the shame and humiliation, but also the grief and helplessness within their shared representations.

In 1878, after much political scheming and many wars, the Serbians (as well as Montenegrins) were declared independent from the Ottoman Empire by the Treaty of Berlin. The treaty, however, placed them under the control of Austria-Hungary, which in turn tried to suppress Serbia's

Kosovo spirit. Serbia soon found itself in the Balkan Wars of 1912–1913, but was finally able to "liberate" Kosovo after over 500 years. A young soldier later recalled this liberation:

> ... The single sound of that word—Kosovo—caused an indescribable excitement. This one word pointed to the black past—five centuries. In it exists the whole of our sad past—the tragedy of Prince Lazar and the entire Serbian people ...
>
> Each of us created for himself a picture of Kosovo while we were still in the cradle. Our mothers lulled us to sleep with the songs of Kosovo, and in our schools our teachers never ceased in their stories of Lazar and Miloš.
>
> My God, what awaited us! To see a liberated Kosovo ... When we arrived on Kosovo ... the spirits of Lazar, Miloš and all the Kosovo martyrs gaze on us. (From *Vojincki Glasnik*, June 28, 1932, in Emmert, 1990, pp. 133–134)

Such identification with the martyrs of Kosovo was an attempt to reverse humiliation and helplessness.

Less than two years after Kosovo's liberation, on St. Vitus Day of 1914, a Bosnian Serb named Gavrilo Princip assassinated Archduke Franz Ferdinand and his pregnant wife in Sarajevo, thereby signaling the beginning of World War I. What is known about Princip is that as a teenager he, as most other Serbian youngsters, was filled with the transformed images of Lazar and Miloš as avengers (Emmert, 1990). Although Serbia was now "free", the Austro-Hungarian Empire exerted significant influence over much of the region after the Ottomans. In Princip's mind, it appears that the old and new "oppressors" were condensed, and the desire for revenge was transferred to the Austro-Hungarian heir apparent.

After World War I, the attempt to bring all the South Slavs into one kingdom slowly succeeded and the kingdom of the Serbs, Croats, and Slovenes was founded, later to be known as Yugoslavia, which means "land of the Southern Slavs"—distinguishing them from northern Slavs such as Poles, Slovakians, and Romanians. Yugoslavia was formed of five "lands": Serbia, Montenegro, Slovenia, Croatia, and Bosnia. As one might expect, the kingdom was fragmented by frequent quarrels. In 1941 Yugoslavia surrendered to the Nazis, and while what happened in the Nazi period is another story, which tells much about the present-day, open or hidden, Serbian-Croat-Muslim enmities, I will not dwell on it here.

In 1945 Yugoslavia was reorganised as a Communist state with Marshall Josip Broz Tito as its head. The new Yugoslavia included the original five "lands", now called republics, plus Macedonia. Kosovo and Vojvodina, in southern and northern Serbia, respectively, remained "autonomous" republics. Under the Communist regime in Yugoslavia, Serbs, Croats, Muslims, Slovenes, Montenegrins, and others lived together in relative peace, although this was not the case at all times. For example, in the late 1960s and early 1970s Croat nationalists demanded the formation of an independent Croatia. To combat such problems, the Communists attempted to create a "Yugoslav man" similar to the Soviet ideal of "Soviet man" in which all peoples were considered equal and connected through the higher objectives of Communist ideology. Prince Lazar's representation was officially degraded as a "symbol of reactionary nationalism" (Kaplan, 1993, p. 39), and in Bosnia-Herzegovina, for example, more than one-quarter of all marriages were mixed and less than three per cent of all Muslims attended prayers in a mosque (Vulliamy, 1994). But we now know that each group in Yugoslavia held strongly on to its own identity rather than becoming part of a single "Yugoslavian" people. After Mikhael Gorbachev's introduction of *glasnost* and *perestroika* in 1987 in the Soviet Union, the Socialist Republic of Yugoslavia began to shake: each group began to ask "Who are we now?" and "How are we different from others?"

In April 1987, Slobodan Milošević, then a Communist bureaucrat, was attending a meeting of 300 party delegates in Kosovo. At the time only ten per cent of the population in Kosovo was Serbian; the majority was Albanian Muslim. During the meeting a crowd of Serbs (and also Montenegrins) tried to force their way into the meeting hall. They wanted to express their grievances about the hardships they were experiencing in Kosovo. The local police blocked and prohibited the crowd's entry into the meeting hall. At that moment, Milošević stepped forward and said: "Nobody, either now or in the future, has the right to beat you." The crowd responded in a frenzy, spontaneously began singing "Hej Sloveni", the national anthem, and shouted "We want freedom! We will not give up Kosovo!" In turn, Milošević was excited; he stayed in the building until dawn—for thirteen hours—listening to the tales of victimisation and the wish to reverse shame, humiliation, and helplessness. Milošević came out of this experience wearing the "armour" of

Serbian nationalism. In a speech, he would later declare that Serbs in Kosovo are not a minority since "Kosovo is Serbia and will always be Serbia."

Before reporting how Milošević and his associates launched a propaganda machine to reactivate the Serbian chosen trauma and effect time collapse I will summarise my findings on Milošević's life and inner world. He came from a dysfunctional family, the second son born to an Orthodox priest during the Nazi occupation of 1941. He experienced numerous severe traumas in his early years: when he was seven, his favorite uncle, an army officer, killed himself with a bullet to the head. When he was twenty-one his father did the same. When he was in his early thirties, his mother, a school teacher and communist, hung herself in the family sitting room (Vulliamy, 1994).

He married his teenage sweetheart, Mirjana Marković, but this story is no fairytale either. Like Milošević, Mirjana had a traumatic childhood. Her mother, accused of divulging information about Partisans while she was under arrest by the Nazis, was executed by the Communists after World War II. There was a widespread belief that Mirjana's maternal grandfather played a role in the execution of his daughter.

My investigations led me to the conclusion that Milošević and his wife had developed a kind of "twinning" psychology. This term means that two people share certain ego functions and/or perform such functions for the other, the "twin", in order to escape internal conflicts, mostly internalised object conflicts (Volkan & Ast, 1997). In the psyches of Milošević and his wife there seemed to be basic trust problems and unfinished issues, rage, and dependency concerning people who were dead.

Milošević was not known to have many other lasting and trusting relationships. Through both secondary sources as well as personal interviews with individuals who knew him, I have concluded that he exhibited characteristics of a narcissistic personality organisation mixed with schizoid characteristics. He was presented to me as an aloof, humorless, calculating, and self-centered person. He seemed determined to remain "number one" at almost any cost, including the destruction of others. A saying in Belgrade went something like this: "Have pity on the person whom Milošević has called a friend." The former German ambassador to Yugoslavia, Horst Grabert, knew Milošević well. When I spoke with him in November 1995 in Berlin he also confirmed that Milošević was a loner and had no genuine Serbian friends. It is possible that for his own personal reasons Milošević wanted to wear the "armour" of nationalism, the large-group identity, in order to hide his traumatised parts. He became the president of Serbia in 1989.

Clinical work with individuals indicates that persons who have experienced drastic losses associated with extreme aggression as it appears in suicide and who have become stuck in complicated mourning tend to "resurrect", symbolically or in actions, the dead and their substitutes in an attempt to mourn, although this process never has an adaptive end for them. Milošević was such a person. The libidinal wish to repair the image of the loss and the aggressive wish to "kill" (psychologically bury) it seem doomed to alternate repeatedly. Most people who suffer from complicated mourning go through these kinds of repetitions without initiating drastic societal or political processes, or massive destructive actions. In Milošević's case, however, his complicated mourning dovetailed with his narcissistic personality organisation. This background may explain why Milošević played a key role in bringing Lazar back to "life" in an omnipotent way and facilitated "killing" him again by having "funerals" in every Serbian town.

One story in particular illustrates how Milošević brought Lazar to "life". About one year after Lazar's execution, a tomb in Ravanica monastery in Kosovo was completed for his body and he was declared a saint. As the "myths" of Lazar spread, numerous icons began to appear in Serbian churches and monasteries in which he was depicted as a Christ-like figure. Decades later, just prior to Ottoman rule coming to Ravanica, Lazar's remains were moved to Frushka Gora, northwest of Belgrade. In 1889, the 500th anniversary of Kosovo, plans for moving Lazar's mummified body back to Ravanica were discussed, but never materialised. As the 600th anniversary approached, however, Milošević and others in his circle were determined to bring Lazar's body out of "exile". The mummified body was placed in a coffin and taken "on tour" to every Serbian village and town, where he was received by huge crowds of mourners dressed in black. Because of this "time collapse" of 600 years, initiated by Serbian leadership, Serbs began to feel that the defeat in Kosovo had occurred only yesterday, an outcome made far easier by the fact that the "chosen trauma" had been kept alive throughout the centuries. (I want to remind the reader that I am obviously making a generalisation here—those who maintained their individualised identities would not be influenced by political propaganda.) As the

Serbs greeted Lazar's body, they cried and wailed and gave speeches saying that they would never allow such a defeat to occur again.

What interests us here is that Milošević apparently reactivated Lazar's representation in the Serbs' minds so that mourning losses due to his defeat at the Battle of Kosovo could at last be accomplished, and the reversal of helplessness, humiliation, and shame could be completed. In any case, affects pertaining to traumatised self-representations were felt freshly; sharing this invisibly connected Serbs more closely and they began to develop similar self-representations in which there was a drastic change: a new sense of entitlement for revenge.

Milošević continued to stir nationalist sentiments. For instance, he ordered the building of a huge monument/memorial on a hill overlooking the Kosovo battlefield. Made of red stone, representing blood (Kaplan, 1993), it stands 100 feet over the "grieving" flowers, and is surrounded by artillery shell-shaped cement pillars inscribed with a sword and the dates 1389–1989. On the tower are written Lazar's words before the battle calling every Serbian man to come to the Field of Black Birds to fight the Turks. If a Serb fails to respond to this call, Lazar's words warn: "He will not have a child, neither male or female, and he will not have fertile land where crops grow." By building the monument and linking 1389 with 1989 (a concrete example of "time collapse") Milošević was resending Lazar's ancient message to the present. The message to the Serbian men was clear: "Either you fight against the Turks or be castrated!"

On 28 June 1989, the 600th anniversary of the Battle of Kosovo, a helicopter brought Milošević to the Field of the Black Birds. He "took the podium from dancing maidens in traditional folk costume and transported the crowd to heights of frenzied adoration with a simple message: 'never again would Islam subjugate the Serbs'" (Vulliamy, 1994, p. 51). In one photo of this rally I noted that Lazar's ancient call to battle against the Turks was imprinted on the T-shirts of many of those present. Riding this wave of nationalism, Milošević's prominence increased. In 1990 the six Yugoslav republics held elections in which the Communists were defeated everywhere except Serbia and Montenegro. In Serbia the Communists were now called the Serbian Socialist Party, and Milošević was elected as party head. In 1991 Milošević summoned Radovan Karadzić, the Bosnian Serbs' leader, and others to meet with him to discuss the future of the republics. In June 1992, after disposing of his "friend" and mentor Ivan Stambolić, then the State President, whom he had accused of betraying the Serbs in Kosovo, Milošević was elected president of the third "Yugoslavia" (the Serb-Montenegrin federation).

Meanwhile, Turks (Ottomans) once more became the "clear and present" enemy (see: also Anzulovic, 1999). When I interviewed University of Virginia graduate Hasan Aygün, who had run the Turkish embassy in Belgrade during Milošević's time, he described how he was considered "public enemy number one" in the Serbian capital city. Everywhere he went Serbs asked him "Why are you [Turks] planning to invade us?" Aygün thought that many Serbs believed in the imminence of a Turkish invasion, and he literally feared for his safety because of the "time collapse" there. One of his observations interested me. He said that many Serbian youngsters had developed a new game: playing Russian roulette with pistols loaded with live ammunition. Many of these teenagers died or were hospitalised with head wounds. This shared new "game" suggested to me identification or attempted identification with Lazar's representation carried through generations. Like Lazar, these youngsters were experiencing two choices: death/ martyrdom or life/revenge on Turks.

The Bosnian Muslims were now experienced by the Serbs as the extension of the Ottomans, and Serbs often referred to them as Turks. There is, of course, a basis of truth to this perception since Bosnian Muslims played a significant role in Ottoman Turkish history. Many Bosnian Muslim epic songs refer to their chosen glories under the Ottomans (Butler, 1993). Within the emotional atmosphere resulting from a time collapse, the Serbs, especially those living in Bosnia-Herzegovina, began to feel entitled to do to Bosnian Muslims what they believed the Ottoman Turks had done to them (Anzulovic, 1999).

Before the ethnic cleansing and systematic rape of Bosnian Muslim women began, Serbian propaganda increasingly focused on inflaming the idea that the Ottomans, now symbolised by the Bosnian Muslims, would return. One piece of propaganda against Bosnian Muslims read:

> By order of the Islamic fundamentalist from Sarajevo, healthy Serbian women from 17 to 40 years of age are being separated out and subjected to special treatment. According to their sick plans going back many years, these women have to be impregnated by orthodox Islamic seeds in order to raise a generation of janissaries

> [Ottoman troops] on the territory they surely consider to be theirs,
> the Islamic republic. In other words, a fourfold crime is to be com-
> mitted against the Serbian woman: to remove her from her own
> family, to impregnate her by undesirable seeds, to make her bear a
> stranger and then to take even him away from her. (Gutman, 1993)

This propaganda aimed to create fear among Serbs that the Bosnian
Muslims intended to resurrect the *devşirme* and create a new janissary
army. There is a kernel of truth in this idea since Bosnian Muslim leader
Alija Izetbegović had intimated in speeches and writings the possibility
of an Islamic enterprise in Bosnia for which he sought the help of other
fundamentalist elements in Muslim countries.

The fear equating Bosnian Muslims with Ottoman Turks was based
on fantasy, however, for the former had virtually no military power.
Yet the massive externalisation and projection of Serbs' aggression onto
the Bosnian Muslims was so great that it began to "boomerang"—they
perceived a "real" threat, based on their chosen trauma and time collapse, and felt compelled to act against it. Thus, the collective idea that
Muslims had to be exterminated slowly began to occur. The Serbs emotionally prepared themselves to "purify" their identity in a malignant
way from any possibility of contamination by the Ottoman Turks/
Bosnian Muslims.

Sarajevo housed many buildings, works of art and manuscripts that
reflected the city's past under the Ottomans. A precious Quran, given
by the Grand Vizier Mehmed Pasha, was featured in the city's famous
Gazi Husrev-Beg library. What is interesting is that many Bosnian Serbs
who bombarded Sarajevo were from the Bosnian capital itself (Butler,
1993). In their collective regression and response to "time collapse", the
city needed to be "purified" of any Muslim connection.

The reactivation of the Serbian chosen trauma and "reincarnating",
"re-killing", and "playing" with a dead person's (in reality, Prince
Lazar's) remains was planned as a rationalisation for atrocities. Other
Serbs in power, such as Radovan Karadžic and Ratko Miladić, then used
the same rationalisation for their actions. In December 1994, former
United States president Jimmy Carter went to Bosnia-Herzegovinia in
the hope of stopping the bloodshed, and met with Karadžic and Miladić.
My colleague from the Carter Center, Joyce Neu was present. According to Neu (personal communication with author), instead of talking
about urgent issues at hand, Karadžic and Miladić used the meeting to

speak about the 1389 Serbian chosen trauma, Serbian victimisation, and their need to protect their large group.

In conjunction with the shared fantasy that Muslims must be cleansed or exterminated was also the shared fantasy that the *devşirme* must be reversed—that the number of Serbs must also be increased to carry on the battle. Hence a conscious strategy of intimidation was condensed with an unconscious one, resulting in the systematic rape of thousands of Muslim women by Serbian soldiers. The underlying assumption of the Serbs was that the child produced by the rape of a non-Serb woman would be a Serb, and not carry any of the traits of the mother. Questioning this belief, Allen (1996) noted, "Enforced pregnancy as a method of genocide makes sense only if you are ignorant about genetics. No baby born from such a crime will be only Serb. It will receive half its genetic material from its mother" (p. 80). This fact hardly seems to need explanation, yet the author was clearly focusing on logical thinking and biological reality, and in the case of inflamed ethnic animosities, it is the "psychological truth" that holds more importance.

Thus Serbs sought to both kill young Muslim men and replace them with new "Serb" children and truly avenge Kosovo. Fact and fantasy, past and present, were intimately and violently intermingled. The Srebrenica massacre occurred in July 1995. More than 8,000 Bosnian Muslim men and boys were rounded up and murdered as the Serbs called them "Turks".

The International Criminal Tribunal for the Former Yugoslavia was created in 1993, and the court spent $200 million to try Milošević on charges of sixty-six counts of crimes against humanity, genocide in Croatia, Bosnia, and Kosovo during the 1990s. On 11 March 2006, Milošević was found dead, due to natural causes, in his cell at the United Nations detention center in The Hague. On 26 February 2007 the court found that there was no evidence linking Milošević to the crime of genocide in the Bosnian War. However, it was stated that Milošević (and others in Serbia) did not do enough to prevent acts of genocide from occurring, particularly in Srebrenika. Psychological understanding of a chosen trauma, its reactivation and concept of "time collapse" are not part of a legal process.

By writing about Bosnia-Herzegovina I do not mean to reduce what happened there to the reactivation of a chosen trauma, inflaming Christoslavism, and time collapse only. But I do want to emphasise that knowing about psychological processes, especially the unconscious processes, can expand our understanding of how they may become the fuel that ignites the most horrible human dramas and/or keep the fire going once hostilities start. Psychoanalytic research into the transgenerational transmission of shared trauma and its activation in leader-follower relationships may illuminate many hidden aspects of ethnic or other large-group conflicts and tell us how internal and external world issues become intertwined.

When I presented the story of the most recent reactivation of the Serbian chosen trauma at professional meetings I received some negative notes from my Serbian psychoanalyst and psychotherapist friends. This is very understandable. I use this example because I studied it carefully over several years and I believe it illustrates some concepts concerning large-group psychology in its own right very clearly. Otherwise, working in many parts of the world, I have come to the firm conclusion that individual and large-group psychology of human beings, whatever large-group identity they may have, are the same everywhere.

CHAPTER TEN

Intertwining old "memories" and affects with current ones

Psychoanalysts have long known that, when an event stirs up intense emotions in an individual, this person will tend to recall past events associated with the same emotions and will sometimes get involved in new events that induce these same emotions again. Sometime such past events are those that took place before the person's own birth, their images having been passed down through generations. When the event and what it stirs up are shared, communities and large groups' common feelings, fears, and mental defences against these fears express themselves in political, social, or cultural actions and processes. In the previous chapter I described the reactivation of a firmly established chosen trauma. Chosen traumas can be reactivated with the aim of supporting the large group's narcissistic investment in large-group identity with accompanying "bad" externalisations and projections on the Other without leading to human tragedies, and sometimes, as described in the previous chapter, with massive traumas. Besides reactivation of established chosen traumas, large groups under the influence of certain events sometimes go back into their histories and intertwine historical "memories" and associated affects with current political issues. This chapter provides an example of this intertwining.

I had the honour of being an Inaugural Yitzhak Rabin Fellow at the Yitzhak Rabin Center for Israel Studies in Tel Aviv beginning in February 2000. My office was in a building near Tel Aviv University, the temporary location of the Yitzhak Rabin Center. The permanent building for the Yitzhak Rabin Center would be opened in November 2005, on the tenth anniversary of Rabin's assassination. I lived in an apartment facing the Mediterranean Sea about half a block from the American Embassy. On the afternoon of 26 March 2000, I stepped out for a breath of fresh air on the balcony of my Tel Aviv apartment and noticed an unusual flurry of activity across the street on the beach promenade below. From my vantage point on the third floor, I watched as a podium was erected and surrounded by loudspeakers, and then a huge balloon on which was written, "The Nation is with Golan" in Hebrew rose from the beach. As the crowd grew larger and larger, the number of police restricting it from spilling out into the street toward the American Embassy also increased. Just before the sun disappeared into the Mediterranean Sea behind the crowd, the popular music that had been playing was hushed and emotional speeches began. From my perspective, the effect was rather like an illusion of waves on dry land, as the protestors, waving flags and slogan-covered banners, seemed to surge with excitement in response. As darkness set in, I watched the unusual scene below as people lit hundreds of torches. But the music, more militant now, reminded me that the people under my balcony were not there to amuse themselves on the beach. On the contrary, they were deadly serious: they were there to influence public opinion, and perhaps most importantly, to warn then-Prime Minister Ehud Barak that he would be a traitor in their eyes if he "gave up" the Golan Heights to Syria. At this time the United States President Bill Clinton was actively seeking a "solution" to the Middle East conflict. Over the course of several hours, some in the crowd made a few attempts to break the police line and stop traffic on Herbert Samuel Street in front of the American Embassy. But the police kept order, and, after a time, the rally came to a peaceful end. Nevertheless, what I had observed during the late afternoon and early evening on 26 March reminded me that the intensity of emotions during this rally was also linked to a generalised surge of emotions tied to the Israeli sentiment that is usually expressed with the phrase "never again".

Pope John Paul II's historic visit to Israel that began on 21 March had ended the day the rally I observed took place under my Tel Aviv balcony. The pope's visit had returned many Israelis' attention to an array of past incidents in which Jews were victimised by Christians. I did not observe or hear about any psychological preparation of the public in Israel for his visit. Although on the surface the Israeli public appreciated John Paul II's gestures of contrition and conciliation, it was clear to me that, for many, his presence also rekindled feelings associated with past persecutions.

One of the past events that the Pope's visit revivified in many Israelis' imaginations was the mid-nineteenth century case of Edgardo Mortara and the quick-tempered Pope Pius IX ("Pio Nono"), as was apparent from the newspaper articles written during the March 2000 visit and in discussions I heard among my Israeli colleagues at the Rabin Center. In 1856, Edgardo, a four-year-old Jewish child, lay gravely ill in his family's home in Bologna. Probably expecting Edgardo's death, a Catholic servant secretly baptised the ailing boy. But Edgardo recovered. Two years later, when the members of the Bologna Inquisition board learned of the secret baptism, they decided that something had to be done. A boy who had been baptised a Christian could not be raised in a Jewish home. In June 1858, papal guards with orders from Pius IX kidnapped Edgardo from the home of his parents, Momolo and Marianna Mortara, in the middle of the night. As might be expected, his family was devastated. Pleas for the boy's return poured in from leading figures in Great Britain, France, Austria, and the United States, from Austrian Emperor Franz Joseph to philanthropist Moses Montifiore to Napoleon III; the *New York Times* alone ran twenty editorials urging the pope to return the child. But Pio Nono would not restore Edgardo to his family, and eventually he actually adopted the boy himself. Edgardo lived the rest of his life as a Catholic and died in Belgium in 1940 at the age of 88, just two months before the Nazi invasion (Kertzer, 1997; Wills, 2000).

It is not accidental that Edgardo Mortara's case was much revived in the Israeli press during John Paul's March 2000 visit to Israel, because the pope was expected to announce the formal beatification of Pio Nono about six months later. In fact, the beatification took place on 3 September 2000. Though John Paul II aimed to heal old Catholic-Jewish wounds, the recollection of the Edgardo Mortara case and the upcoming beatification of the "kidnapper pope" kept those wounds bleeding (Davis, 2000; Henry, 2000; Smith, 2000). That the pope's gestures and remarks fell short of an actual apology for the Vatican's relationship with the Nazis during World War II probably did not help matters.

At the same time, religious-secular relations, as well as those between Ashkenazim Jews who originally came from Eastern Europe and Russia, and Sephardim Jews who originally came from the Iberian Peninsula, took a turn for the worse as Ehud Barak's coalition government seemed on the verge of coming apart. The papal visit to Israel coincided with the timing of an intemperate attack by Rabbi Ovadia Yosef, spiritual leader of the Orthodox Sephardim party Shas (then the largest component of Barak's coalition after the prime minister's own Labour Party) on then-Education Minister Yossi Sarid, a member of the liberal/secular Meretz party, the third-largest segment of the government at that time. Upset by Sarid's attitude towards funding for the Shas school system, Yosef compared the minister to Haman and Amalek, Biblical enemies of the Jewish people. During the weekly broadcast, Yosef proceeded to curse Sarid and called on God to blot out the minister's memory, leading then-Israeli Attorney General Elyakim Rubinstein to investigate Rabbi Yosef for incitement. Yosef supporters, orthodox Sephardim activists, warned that massive violence would erupt should police try to question the Shas spiritual leader. On the night of 27 March, some 2,000 Shas activists rallied outside mentor Rabbi Ovadia Yosef's home in Jerusalem's Har Nof neighbourhood, and the party leader called Attorney General Rubinstein a "racist". There were reports, however, suggesting that Rabbi Yosef's attack on the Education Minister Sarid had in fact been supported by some Ashkenazi rabbis and political figures (Keinon, 2000). Barak's coalition was, to say the least, severely threatened. I must add that soon after the 27 March 2000 rally, it became clear that the Shas would not leave the coalition, despite the heated rhetoric. The Shas did eventually did withdraw from the government in early July 2000, when it became evident that Ehud Barak, as well as Yasser Arafat, would attend a critical Middle East peace summit convened by President Bill Clinton at Camp David, Maryland. On 10 July 2000, Barak narrowly survived a no-confidence vote in the Knesset: fifty-two votes for and fifty-four against, with sixty-one votes needed to topple his government. On that day, Barak flew to Washington after a heavily guarded ceremony at Ben Gurion Airport. Before long, Barak was defeated by Ariel Sharon in the general elections.

Returning to the Pope's visit, John Paul II departed Israel on 26 March, leaving Israelis with mixed emotions, and not merely because the visit had dredged up memories of relatively distant past conflicts between Jews and Christians. The pope's visit had also prompted a more explicit than usual review of Jewish-Muslim issues in Israel at that time. Discussions at the Rabin Center among Israeli colleagues also clearly illustrated this. Palestinians had worked hard to make their presence felt during the papal tour of the Holy Land. The pope had met with Yasser Arafat—then the president of the Palestinian Authority (the self-rule agency responsible for education, social welfare, health, tourism, and taxation in some Palestinian areas)—during the visit to the holy areas under the jurisdiction of the Palestinian authority. Thus, President Bill Clinton's meeting in Geneva on the day of the Pope's departure with then-Syrian President Hafez al-Assad was like turning up the heat when the water was already boiling.

Lurie's "NewsCartoon" in *The Jerusalem Post* that day pictured Assad and Clinton sitting face to face at a table, a cooked dove, symbol of peace, missing one leg, lying on a plate between them. Assad is in the process of eating the detached leg of the dove; the caption reads: "As you can see, President Clinton, I *love* peace!" For many Israelis, the notion of peace with Syria implied the likelihood of losing the Golan Heights, which was taken by Israel from Syria during the 1967 war. This prospect, in turn, generated increased emotions. The summit between Clinton and Assad was especially anxiety-provoking for the 18,000 Israeli residents of the Golan, some of whom were still invested in the homes and vineyards there though they lived in apprehension about the future. In the emotional atmosphere surrounding the pope's visit— the talk of the possible collapse of the Barak government, the Assad-Clinton summit, and revivified images of the World War II Vatican and the 1858 Edgardo Mortara case inflaming the pre-existing religious-secular split—dozens of buses carrying Golan residents arrived in Tel Aviv on the afternoon of 26 March. Altogether, about 2,000 people assembled on the promenade between the beach and the street that runs in front of the American Embassy to protest Clinton's effort to facilitate peace talks between Syria and Israel, and to blame Barak for, as the opposition Likud party chairman Ariel Sharon (who would be elected prime minister on 6 February 2001) wrote in *The Jerusalem Post* that day, "ceding everything to Syria without any real return", while "ripping the nation to shreds."

This was the demonstration that I happened to observe from my balcony. By the next day, it was clear that the Assad-Clinton summit had been a failure, and discussions about the Golan's future were shelved. The main political reason for the failure of the Assad-Clinton summit was, as I was told, the fact that Assad refused to show any flexibility regarding Syria's demand that Israel withdraw from the entire

Golan Heights. Israel was reportedly willing to offer withdrawal from additional territories in order to keep the complete shoreline of the Sea of Galilee, which is Israel's primary source of fresh water, but Assad would not budge. Hafez al-Assad died from heart failure on 11 June 2000, aged sixty-nine, and was succeeded by his son Bashar who, as I am writing this book, is in the news concerning his brutality against his own people.

The memory of the rally I had watched for over three hours from my balcony seemed to evaporate in the next day's early mist; by morning, the beach and the promenade were already cleared of the rubbish the crowd had left behind, and Tel Aviv residents were out running and strolling on the beach, returning the place to routine and normalcy. However, what I observed from my balcony the day before, combined with what I read in the newspapers and heard—from colleagues at the Rabin Center and other persons, ranging from the Minister of Immigrant Absorption to Yitzhak Rabin's wife and sister, to Israeli historians and psychologists—bore witness to the intertwining of past historical "memories" linked to certain affects with internal and external politics.

I finished my tenure in Tel Aviv at the end of May 2000. Just before I left, there were signs of obvious anxiety among those at the temporary building that housed the Rabin Center. For example, when I went there one morning I heard a "joke" about how Barak went to a wedding party secretly, but a photographer found him anyway and took his picture from a distance. The idea behind this "joke" was that if a photographer could find the prime minister and take his picture, an assassin also could find him and shoot him. Nervous laughter would follow such "jokes". Public response to the killing of Yitzhak Rabin also seemed to be reactivated. Soon after I left Israel the second Intifada started. In the safety of my home in Virginia I watched the horrors of suicide bombings on television. Meanwhile, President Clinton continued his attempts to bring lasting peace between Israelis and Palestinians until he left the White House on 20 January 2001. Eventually, Israelis and Palestinians met in Taba in the Sinai from 21 January to 27 January 2001 to discuss what they could do with the so-called "Clinton Parameters". Their meeting ended without an agreement. Ariel Sharon was elected to become the new Israeli prime minister in February. Bullets, bombs, and killing in the name of identity would continue, including suicide bombings, the focus of the next chapter.

CHAPTER ELEVEN

Political propaganda, suicide bombers, and terrorism

A s the former Yugoslavian example described in Chapter Nine illustrates, when a large group is regressed and people wonder, "Who are we now?" the personality of the political leader may become an important factor in the scenario, one that has considerable influence on societal and political processes. He or she may inflame or tame ethnic or other large-group sentiments.

A destructive leader, usually with narcissistic personality organisation, may aim to enhance and/or modify the large group's "new" identity by oppressing or even destroying, one way or another, an unwanted group within the legal boundaries of a state or an enemy outside the boundaries. In a step-by-step process, destructive leaders and their propaganda machines enhance a shared sense of victimisation within the large group. This may be following an attack by an enemy group or another disaster, such as an economic one, or even in situations without any visible recent victimisation, and may include reactivation of a chosen trauma or a past shared trauma, and creation of a time collapse that mixes up the image of a past enemy with the present devalued group within the legal boundary or the new "enemy" outside. This increases a sense of "we-ness" (large-group narcissism) contaminated with an entitlement ideology. The large group may turn the entitlement ideology into revengeful actions and malignant purification. Under certain circumstances the large group, without realistic means to be "sadistic" towards the current enemy, may idealise its own victimisation and become omnipotently "masochistic", feeling entitled to provoke self-punishment contaminated with hope for revenge.

Major Milovan Milutinović was one key figure in running the Serbian propaganda machine under the Milošević regime. In 1991, he was interviewed by American journalist Roy Gutman who was so shocked by references to the Ottoman Janissaries that he asked Milutinović, "Which century are you talking about?" (Gutman, 1993, p. x). Milutinović responded that it was a recent phenomenon, adding, "They are trying to do what they did centuries ago" (Gutman, 1993, p. x). In Milutinović's statement we hear references to the consequences of the reactivation of the Serbian chosen trauma, a time collapse, and an example of equating the past enemy with the current one and equating a fantasy with reality. I have no way of knowing if Milutinović really believed what he was saying. The important issue is that his remarks were an aspect of a large-group phenomenon that was dominated by the psychology of time collapse in a regressed society and was induced by malignant political propaganda.

Political propaganda exists in all politically organised large groups. The historical precursors to it may be the tribal battle sounds of earlier times. The ancient war-cry, called *alala*, accompanied by non-verbal symbols such as banners and uniforms, is said to have been a significant factor for the Greeks and for their enemies. The ancient Roman armies used shouts and accompanying trumpet blasts, called, *clamor*, and later adapted the Teutonic battle-cry, *barditus*: "Tacitus describes it as an explosion of raucous sounds, made more prolonged and more resounding by pressing the shield against the mouth" (Chakotin, 1939, p. 34). Beginning as a murmur, it would steadily increase into a roar, rousing the soldiers to intense excitement.

As human history proceeded, the appearance of propaganda in its broader sense became more closely connected with religious issues. In 1622, *Sacra Congregatio de Propaganda Fide* (the "Sacred Congregation for Propagating the Faith" of the Roman Catholic Church) was established by the Vatican. The term "propaganda" thus became pejorative in Protestant Western Europe because it was associated with the project of spreading Catholicism in the New World at the expense of and in opposition to the "reformed" faiths. Christians used religion as a tool for propaganda and for protecting religious investment (Jowett & O'Donnell, 1992). The battle cry of the Muslim Ottoman Empire was simply their God's name, as if their battles were sanctioned by God and any Ottoman soldier killed in battle would be cared for by Him; Ottoman Janissaries shouted "Allah! Allah!" as their colourful marching band, the *Mehter*, provided exciting background music.

According to historian Lewis (2000), political propaganda in its modern sense did not begin until after the French Revolution (1789–1799). Before then, there was essentially no meaningful contact between the rulers and the ordinary people. Those in power had no need to communicate with or manipulate the public; they simply ruled.

When Franz Anton Mesmer, a Viennese physician, appeared on the European scene at the beginning of the nineteenth century with his new "science" called hypnotism, a theoretical explanation for political propaganda was found. Gustave Le Bon, a French social psychologist who was born two decades after Mesmer's death, published *The Crowd, a Study of Popular Mind* that echoed the dynamics of hypnotism (Le Bon, 1895). Le Bon held that a person in a group loses much individual distinctiveness and acts in accordance with the group's consensual urges. The effects are readily apparent. Without carefully differentiating small groups—in which participants see and get to know one another—from large groups, Le Bon noted that crowds crave illusions. The leader can supply such illusions much like a hypnotist.

Freud's psychoanalytic ideas about large groups were influenced by Le Bon's study of the crowd (Freud, 1921c). However, Le Bon's influence on the development of modern malignant propaganda is not common knowledge among psychoanalysts. After visiting India he developed an idea that the white race might be in danger, and in his book *La Psychologie Politique et la Défense Sociale* (Le Bon, 1910), he created a kind of blueprint for fascism.

The discovery of propaganda "by both the man in the street and the man in the study" took place during World War I (1914–1918) (Lasswell, 1938, p. v). When the war began there was no public outcry about oppressed large groups, and no interest in secret diplomacies; the war was fought by professional soldiers who required little knowledge of why they were fighting. But as the war dragged on and began to affect peoples' lives more intimately, there appeared a dual need to stimulate the soldiers' will to fight and to explain the need for privation to the public at home. In order to justify the cost of operations it became necessary to inflate the fruits of victory with vague, but lofty-sounding, notions such as "self determination" and "the war to end all wars" (Brown, 1963, p. 91). Thus, Lasswell (1938, p. v) argued, propaganda was "discovered".

In World War I, besides printed material, telegrams and the wireless were routinely available to influence the masses. Though motion pictures were still a relatively new technology in the second decade of the twentieth century, their use for propaganda purposes nevertheless began during this war as well. Germany came late to deploying movies as a means of propaganda; the German propaganda was ineffectual during World War I. During World War II, however, an elaborately developed German film propaganda machine reached its apotheosis in the well-known works of Leni Riefenstahl and others.

Adolf Hitler devoted two chapters in *Mein Kampf* to the proper design and execution of political propaganda. It should be aimed "only to a limited degree at the so-called intellect … The art of propaganda lies in understanding the emotional ideas of great masses and finding through a psychologically correct form, the way to attention and hence to the heart of the broad masses" (Hitler, 1925–1926, p. 180). Hitler found an especially talented confederate in Joseph Goebbels who was ultimately responsible for creating Hitler's image and many of his signature gestures. After the political and economic humiliation experienced by the German people, Nazi propaganda created a shared psychic reality in which the "Aryan" identity of the German people was built up, while millions of Jews, and many Roma and other targeted groups were dehumanised and killed.

The main characteristic of Nazi propaganda was to build up the Führer's and the Nazi authorities' omnipotence, and provide satisfaction for the Germans in their belief that they were followers of a mighty leader who would lift up their self-esteem and make them special super beings. Genocide occurred in order to prevent the contamination of super beings by those whom the Nazi propaganda rendered subhuman, like dangerous germs (malignant purification). Personal and shared historical and economic hurts and humiliations within the German society could then be effectively denied. The Nazi propaganda used political ideology instead of religion as a tool. But this requires a closer look. Since Hitler was presented as if he were a God, we really cannot clearly differentiate ideological from religious tools for political propaganda in those of the Nazis (see: Volkan, Ast & Greer, 2002 for an extensive examination of Nazi propaganda).

Contrary to the Nazis', the Allies' propaganda during World War II allowed criticism, even while it stressed the gallantry of military forces and distracted attention from defeat. After World War II, international law tried to specify legal exceptions to freedom of speech. Hate speech that incites racism was banned for example. The United States did not join the other countries in accepting the international law concerning hate speech, since it interferes with the First Amendment of the US Constitution. In the United States hate speech is unregulated unless it is proven that it leads to clear and present danger. On the other hand, in today's Germany even hate speech that harms human dignity can be prosecuted. In Israel some laws go back to the Ottoman period and colonial times and the definition of incitement is connected with rebellious acts; this creates certain legal confusion. In short, propaganda and freedom of speech issues often cause heated legal debates even in democratic societies.

Throughout the world we can always find societies subjected, to one degree or another, to what some consider a "malignant" type of propaganda, "brainwashing", or "thought reform" coming from above—as encountered during the growth of Chinese Communism between 1921 and 1948 and in the German Democratic Republic (see, for example, Lifton, 1989; Bytwerk, 2004). As communication technology evolved, it became a primary tool for political propaganda. For example, Iran's Ayatollah Khomeini depended on long-distance telephone calls and tape recorders to spread his religious fundamentalist revolution. At the present time the internet is available for making propaganda and in our daily lives we are constantly exposed to it.

Since propaganda and manipulation exist in every politically organised society, one can argue that differences between the type of propaganda utilised by the leader and his or her associates in one large group and that of another large group will be only a matter of degree. However, such a comparison is not always fair and becomes problematic when societal crises, ideology, type of government, existing laws, economic conditions, and political and military aims are taken into consideration.

In general, psychoanalysts have not written much about political propaganda during recent decades. However, this topic was studied by Kris (1943–1944), Money-Kyrle (1941), and Glower (1947) during and soon after World War II. Kris reminded us about Le Bon's influence on fascism and Nazi propaganda. When Benito Mussolini came to power in Italy he professed that he was influenced by Le Bon's ideas. In turn, Le Bon, then almost ninety years old, became an admirer of the "new order" in Italy. Kris wrote: "The student of history of ideas will note in Le Bon the parallel with Nietzsche and reaction to Marx, but he will also be able to quote chapter and verse in order to prove how closely state- ment by Le Bon reappears in the concepts of propaganda developed by Hitler and Goebbels" (Kris, 1943, p. 388). In Le Bon's scheme the func- tion of political propaganda is clear: the leader as an orator/hypnotist drives the crowd into submission and promotes its regression.

Kris also described others who are helpful in spreading political propaganda: the "opinion leader"—the doctor, the vicar, the teacher, the barber, the union organiser both inside and outside the frame- work of a political group or institution—and the "wicked agitator"— the person who polarises negative and positive attitudes and projects them towards specific targets while striving for applause (Kris, 1943). In today's world we can say there are "wicked agitators" who utilise television, radio, or other sophisticated communication devices to spread mild or vicious political propaganda. When Kris expressed his opinion about political propaganda decades ago, he could not have imagined today's communication technology and streamlined dissemi- nation of information.

Malignant political propaganda is closely associated with the widespread terrorist activities we face today. The term terror- ism derives from French revolutionary statesman Maximilien de Robespierre's 1785–1794 Reign of Terror during the early days of the French Revolution. It refers to terror coming from above. In this book I have already given some examples of this type of terror, which has historically far exceeded, in the sheer number of its victims, any other form of terror. Today, however, especially with the emergence of extreme fundamentalist Muslim suicide bombers, we are more aware of terror coming from below. In this chapter I will not review various types of terrorism throughout the centuries, but focus on the Muslim suicide bombers of recent decades, and others who cause death and destruction and are under the influence of malignant religious propaganda.

In the early 1990s I studied the training of Muslim suicide bomb- ers in the Middle East (Volkan, 1997, 2013). My findings illustrate that the future suicide bombers were exposed to a special kind of political propaganda designed *just for them* (see also, Hafez, 2006). The typical technique of creating Middle Eastern Muslim suicide bombers included two basic steps: first, the "teachers" found young people whose personal identity was already disturbed and who were seeking an outer "element" to internalise so they could stabilise their internal world. Second, they developed a "teaching method" that "forces" the large-group identity—religious and/or ethnic—into the "cracks" of the person's damaged or subjugated individual identity. Once people became candidates to be suicide bombers, the routine rules and regulations, so to speak, or individual psychology did not fully apply to their patterns of thought and action. Future suicide bombers became agents of the large-group identity and would attempt to repair it for themselves and for other members of the large group. Killing themselves (and their personal identity) and Others (enemies) did not matter; it would not induce personalised superego prohibitions. What mattered in these situations was that the act of bombing (terrorism) brought attention to the large-group identity, protected, and maintained it. The suicide bomber was primarily under the dictates of large-group psychology and not under the influence of the bomber's own individual psychology. Direct and indirect support of this activity came from the fact that many other members of the traumatised large group saw the individual bomber as the carrier of the group's identity. Though Islam forbids suicide, there was no lack of conscious and unconscious approval of Muslim suicide bombers from other members of their communities.

I found that there was little difficulty in finding young men interested in becoming suicide bombers in Gaza and the West Bank. Repeated actual and expected events humiliated youngsters and interfered with their adaptive identifications with their parents because their parents were humiliated as well. The mental representations of external events, the sense of helplessness, and the feeling that they were being treated as less than human created "cracks" in individuals' identities. Reports showed that those who selected "bomber candidates" had developed the expertise to sense whose personal identity "gaps" were most suitable to be filled with elements of the large-group identity. For example, those youngsters who suffered from concrete trauma were more suitable candidates than those suffering from more generalised trauma (concrete trauma consists of the trauma caused by an *actual* humiliating event visited upon that person by the enemy, be it a beating, torture, or loss of a parent).

Most suicide bombers in the Middle East were chosen as teenagers, exposed to special political propaganda, "educated", and then sent off to perform their duty when they were in their late teens or early to mid-twenties. The "education" was most effective when religious elements of the large-group identity were provided as solutions for the personal sense of helplessness, shame, and humiliation. Replacing borrowed elements sanctioned by God for one's internal world made that person omnipotent and supported the individual's narcissism, which was intertwined with large-group narcissism. Hafez (2006) also described powerful messages, mostly religious, coming from the propaganda-makers in Palestinian society to recruit and prepare its suicide bombers. The selected candidates' mission was presented not as "suicide", but as martyrdom. It was also strongly suggested that the religious martyrs would be rewarded by God.

In general, the "education" of the Palestinian youngsters who were candidates to become suicide bombers was most often carried out in small groups. These small groups collectively read the Quran written in Arabic and chanted certain religious scriptures again and again. Unlike most of the Pakistani and Afghan "students" in Pakistani madrasas who were trained to be *mujahideen* in Afghanistan and later prepared as supporters for and leaders of the Taliban, and who did not speak Arabic, the Palestinian "students" were able to understand what they were reading in the Arabic Quran. For this reason their readings were carefully selected. The "teachers" also supplied sacred sounding, but meaningless, phrases to be repeated over and over in chants, such as, "I will be patient until patience is worn out from patience." These kinds of mystical sayings combined with selected verses from the Quran helped to create a "different internal world" for the "students".

Meanwhile, the "teachers" also interfered with the "real world" affairs of the students, mainly by cutting off meaningful communication and other ties to students' families, and by forbidding things such as music and television on the grounds that they might be sexually stimulating. Sex and women could be obtained only after a passage to adulthood. In the case of the "bomber candidates", however, the "passage" was through killing oneself, not a symbolic castration that a "normal" youngster may perform in order to identify with the aggressor (father) and become a "man" himself. The oedipal triumph was allowed only after death. Allah, who was presented as a strict and primitive superego against the derivatives of libidinal drive and a force to be obeyed while the youngster was alive, allowed satisfaction of the libidinal wishes by *houris* (angels) in Paradise. The "teachers" referred to the Prophet Muhammad's instructions to his followers, which some consider one of the earliest examples of "war propaganda", during the Battle of Badr (624CE) as they offered immortality to their students and inductees. Muhammad told his followers they would continue to "live" in Paradise if they died during the battle. The youngsters were told that life continued in paradise, and the death of a suicide bomber was celebrated as a "wedding ceremony", a celebration at which friends and family gathered to celebrate their belief that the dead terrorist was in the loving hands of angels in heaven.

Suicide bomber candidates were instructed not to inform their parents of their missions. No doubt parents in this part of the world at that time could surmise what their children's missions were, but regardless, keeping secrets from family members helped create a sense of power within the youngsters. Secrets induced a false sense of further "separation-individuation" (Mahler & Furer, 1968) as it happens in normal development also during the adolescence passage, symbolising the cutting of dependency ties. The dependency ties for the suicide bombers were replaced as they became carriers or "flags" for the large group.

As time passed, training "bomber candidates" by forming small groups was no longer necessary, as terrorist acts were becoming more "endemic" to Palestinian culture. Therefore, some suicide bombers would have a very short, less organised training. Furthermore, the more stress was placed on a large group, the more the people held on to their large-group identity. When the canvas of the metaphorical large-group tent shakes—this time due to malignant propaganda coming from inside the tent supported by threatening and humiliating activities of the Other outside the tent—the more people under the tent grip their large-group identity. Thus, even "normal" persons could be pushed to become candidates for terrorism.

Islamic schools for children and youth are not a new phenomenon in the Islamic world. For example, before the Ottomans, Seljuk Turks had established an empire in Anatolia. They were great builders, and their principal innovation was the *madrasa* (*medrese*). The madrasa was an establishment for the teaching of the religio-judicial sciences. Urban communities with schools, libraries, fountains, baths, and hospitals were established around madrasas. Today we associate madrasas in Afghanistan, Pakistan, and elsewhere with locations where future extreme fundamentalist Islamic terrorists are brainwashed and trained.

What was different in Pakistani madrasas was that they included training in the service of future violence. Such madrasas existed in Pakistan before Osama bin Laden arrived in neighbouring Afghanistan and before the Taliban took control of parts of that country. The teaching in these madrasas was influenced by Deobandi and Wahabi versions of extreme religious "ideology" (Rashid, 2000). At that time, the training of mostly poor children who attended these madrasas was similar to the training of the Middle Eastern Islamic suicide bombers. The children read the Quran in Arabic for years, but since they did not know Arabic, they had to accept the "interpretation" given to them by their teachers. When they read in Urdu, they were told that the Urdu letter "jeem" stood for jihad; "kaaf" for Kalashnikov, and "khy" for khoon (blood) (Ali, 2001). These were the madrasas funded by the United States and Britain to raise mujahideen to fight the Soviets. The Saudis provided more funds for the expansion of Wahabism. The "graduates" of these madrasas would later create a foundation on which the Taliban and al-Qaeda could stand.

The events of 11 September 2001 caused the media and politicians, as well as the public in the United States and many parts of the world, to begin reporting the existence of a new breed of Islamic fundamentalist suicide terrorists. First of all, these terrorists were not "directly" humiliated Palestinians; they were mostly from Egypt and Saudi Arabia. These reports also said that the "profiles" of those in this new group of terrorists did not fit those of the "standard" suicide bomber. These were generally older, well-educated, and came from wealthy, educated families, while the standard Palestinian suicide attacker was a young, uneducated malcontent who usually came from a poor, traumatised family. In many ways, the hijackers of September 11th (such as Mohammed Atta), all from the Middle East, did appear to belong to a new breed. However, I still believe that the mechanisms for creating standard Islamic fundamentalist suicide bombers apply to the new group of terrorists as well. Under generalised malignant political propaganda they took off their individual garments, pulled down their large group's tent's canvas, and wore it as their garment in order to become killers according to the rules and regulations of large-group psychology. Israeli psychoanalyst Erlich (2013), in his study of the terrorist mind, also sees a need to "re-find" the self by losing it, by allowing it to obliterate its boundaries and merge with a greater entity by internalising an ideology.

At the present time I do not have enough data about the lives of Atta and other September 11th hijackers, some of whom we know did not even realise that they were on a fatal mission until the last minute. Excerpts from a rough translation of a four-page document left behind by some of the hijackers illuminate at least one small corner of al-Qaeda's malignant propaganda, training, and command practices. Besides matter-of-fact advice about concealing their true identities, the document also contains selected references from the Quran that seem to give permission for suicide and to sanction killing enemies in the name of God. Between the lines we can see how these instructions created a *ritual* that mixes "God's words" with practical and very simple instructions for mass murder. "Tightening one's shoes", "washing", and "checking one's weapons"—above and beyond their functional aspects for mission preparations—are easy tasks to perform without much internal conflict. The instructions for "cleaning" and removing grime, filth, mud, and stains, besides making the trainees "good" Muslims (who can only "meet" the divine power when they are "clean"), balance the instructions for the actual "dirty work" of killing oneself, the passengers, the crew aboard the plane, and the people in the targeted building. Thus, the steps of leaving one's apartment to hijack and crash an airplane have been ritualised and made psychologically easy. Of course, I do not know how consciously the hijackers' trainers strategised the instruction of their underlings, but to my mind these instructions alone demonstrate a certain mastery of psychologically effective ritual.

As I write this book, on 13 April 2013, two bombs have exploded in Boston during the Boston Marathon, killing three persons, including an eight-year-old boy, and injuring 264. The authorities are busy finding out what made two brothers, Dzhokhar and Tamerlan Tsarnaev, commit such a horrible crime. More information about them, I believe, will eventually come to light. In general, however, we will find similarities between what motivated them to be killers and what motivated Gavrilo Princip to assassinate Archduke Franz Ferdinand and his pregnant wife in Sarajevo on St. Vitus Day of 1914 as described in Chapter Nine. It is clear to me that we will need to further study large-group psychology in its own right and the influence of malignant political propaganda that turns some persons into "tools" to perform crimes against humanity.

CHAPTER TWELVE

"Unofficial" diplomacy and psychoanalytic large-group psychology

Following the French and American Revolutions, instead of rule by a monarch, people chose the notion of self-determination and the idea of nationalism. The "age of nationalism" was thus born at the end of the eighteenth century and in the nineteenth century became an established concept. The model of nation states was expanded to include other large groups that were liberated from the rule of the Other in what we came to know as colonialism. In the process, modern diplomacy was firmly established as a tool of protocol between nation states. This protocol includes broad elements ranging from providing formal representation and serving as a listening post, to reducing friction in cases of conflict (when advisable), to managing change and creating, drafting, and amending international rules (Barston, 1988).

Psychoanalyst Janine Chasseguet-Smirgel (1996) stated that, although attachment to one's native soil is grounded in history, people are connected to each other by certain conscious feelings and beliefs, and when new nationalistic ideals appeared, they replaced religious feelings and beliefs. She reminded us that while nationalism is associated with universal ideals and liberty it can also be used for racism, totalitarianism, and destruction. She believed that the more nationalism replaced religion and stood in for religious mystical feelings—in other words, the more it performed a function that religion no longer was able to fulfill—the more it had a tendency to become a lethal force. This happened in Germany when the National Socialist Party dominated. After the collapse of the Soviet Union, when many large groups asked "Who are we now?" historian Norman Itzkowitz (2004 personal communication with author; see also Volkan, 2013) suggested that the world had entered an "age of ethnicity." Soon this "new" age would become complicated when terrorism in the name of religion spread and symbolically peaked on 11 September 2001. These developments are forcing us to examine how the practice of official diplomacy has changed.

Even before terrorism was associated with extreme fundamentalist Muslim religion and the "war" against it became a routine part of world events, Abba Eban, an orator and the Foreign Minister of Israel (1966 to 1974), noted in 1983 a decline in the role of ambassadors and foreign policy agencies. He referred to "the age of summitry" as emphasising face-to-face meetings between leaders of opposing nations, thereby altering the function of organs such as departments of state in foreign policy determinations. In 1990 a former United States Assistant Secretary of State, Harold Saunders, who would become an active member of the Center for the Study of Mind and Human Interaction (CSMHI) stated after his retirement that in the twentieth century, two world wars and nuclear weapons made us question the legitimacy of nation states using power unilaterally to pursue their own interests. As he reminded us, we cannot ignore the fact that nation states and other large groups around the world still use force and manipulation to achieve their goals, and that there are malignant leaders as well as insensitive, ignorant and arrogant ones. He wrote however: "While most people do not yet see sovereign states fading away, a growing number observe that national sovereignties are increasingly limited in what they can accomplish by themselves and argue that genuine influence comes less and less from the use of raw power alone—that the nature of power and influence has changed" (Saunders, 1990, p. 3). In many locations in today's world a reversal of what Chasseguet-Smirgel (1996) described has occurred, in that shared religious feelings and beliefs that transcend the boundaries of nation states are replacing nationalistic feelings and beliefs. The continuation of al-Qaeda after the death of Osama bin Laden is one example. This, of course, is influencing how modern diplomacy is practised.

Today several factors have reorganised our thinking about the nature of international relationships: the existence of religious conflicts alongside ethnic conflicts, worldwide terrorism (Volkan & Kayatekin, 2006; Volkan, 2013), as well as incredible developments in communications technology (Arnett, 2002), the ascendancy of an intrusive news media (Seib, 1996), a huge increase in international travel (Held, 1998), the influence of modern forms of globalisation that attempt to promote prosperity and wellbeing for societies but also include prejudice and racism (Çevik, 2003; Stiglitz, 2003; Kinnvall, 2004; Ratliff, 2004; Morton, 2005; Liu & Mills, 2006). Obviously diplomacy still includes negotiations between sovereign nation states, but it also includes talking to and dealing with religious, ethnic, or ideological leaders in official and unofficial ways. We can no longer reduce diplomacy to "correct" and ritualistic protocols. Many of today's international problems have created huge gaps in the physical and psychological borders of nation states; they cannot be dealt with as issues confined only within the boundaries of opposing nation states. This is one of the reasons for the incredible increase of non-governmental organisations (NGOs) tasked with "resolving conflicts" and bringing peace to conflicted areas, sometimes by holding on to a magical wish that it could come true for the whole world! "Conflict resolution" has become the name of a "new" profession, a new business investment. Large-group conflicts (as well as personal ones) are here to stay.

Obviously there are as many thoughtful and useful NGOs as there are those that—as one of my high-level professional diplomat friends once told me—are a most irritating nuisance for the professionals and create unnecessary difficulties in international relations. With very few exceptions, it is my observation that these NGOs' activities do not take psychodynamic processes such as those described in this volume into consideration when they structure their activities. This does not mean, however, that what they do will fail; to obtain good results in creating an atmosphere for more humane and civilised interactions between opposing large groups, the facilitators do not necessarily need to possess and utilise deep psychological insights. But psychoanalytically informed insights about large-group processes, I think, will be most helpful, and even necessary, when there is a need to remove psychological resistances to peaceful coexistence and to separate dangers that are fantasy from the real ones.

As there are huge numbers of religiously tinged tragedies in today's international arena, it is not surprising to note the spread of religiously tinged attempts to "resolve" them. It is as if "good" religion will erase the influence of "bad" religion. There are many efforts to convert forgiveness and apology into political virtue, mostly by depending on Christian religious ideas. Worthington (2001) stated that "Forgiveness is rooted in replacing negative emotions associated with anger, fear, and unforgiveness with positive emotions associated with empathy and perhaps with sympathy, love, compassion, or even romantic love" (p. 37) (see also: Worthington, 2005). Narváez and Díaz (2010) wrote that, "The domains of forgiveness include forgiveness to oneself, as well as divine forgiveness" (p. 215). I was invited to attend three international "forgiveness" meetings during the last decade and noted that "magical thinking" dominated such gatherings. Thinking as a psychoanalyst, I can state that "forgiveness" in a large group cannot take place through magical gestures. Taming feelings about the Other—if we can call this "forgiveness"—can be possible after shared mourning over losses, accompanied by shared experiences supporting large-group narcissism; in other words, only when some difficult shared psychological processes are accomplished.

Meanwhile, theoretical and scientific writings about politics also continued to ignore psychoanalysis. In 2005 Ascher and Hirschfelder-Ascher noted that during the previous quarter century political psychology neglected "the roles of affect, psychological needs, and psychodynamic mechanisms that are crucial for understanding the full complexity of political behavior" (p. ix). They stated: "With notable exceptions, political psychology has focused predominantly on explaining individual or collective political behavior rather than trying to guide policy decisions that would be greatly aided by insights about how people react to symbols, how psychological needs shape their perspectives and predispositions, and how crises can undermine the defenses against destructive behaviors" (p. ix). They very successfully examined Harold D. Lasswell's pioneering work in the mid-twentieth century and tried to extend his ideas in applying psychodynamic theories to politics. In Chapter One I listed some ideas that illustrate the difficulty of collaboration between psychoanalysts and diplomats or political scientists. Ascher and Hirschfelder-Ascher suggested that the difficulty of measuring psychoanalytic findings "scientifically" may be another reason for this. It is difficult or impossible to measure "scientifically" unconscious process and fantasies.

Before completing this volume I will briefly describe a psychoanalytically informed methodology dealing with coexistence of opposing large groups. My interdisciplinary colleagues from the Center for the Study of Mind and Human Interaction (CSMHI) and I evolved a multi-year process to apply our findings on large groups and international relations, which have been explored in this volume, to some conflicted areas in the world. Nicknamed the "Tree Model" to reflect the slow growth and branching of a tree, this methodology has three basic components or phases: (1) psychopolitical diagnosis of a situation, (2) psychopolitical dialogues between influential delegates of opposing large groups, and (3) collaborative actions and institutions that grow out of the dialogue process. Since I have discussed the Tree Model in detail elsewhere, with illustrations of its various aspects (Volkan, 1988, 2006a, 2011, 2013), here I will only provide a very brief summary.

The first phase includes in-depth psychoanalytically informed interviews with a wide range of the large group's members from high-level politicians to school children, conducted by the interdisciplinary facilitating team of psychoanalysts, former diplomats, political scientists, historians, and others from different disciplines. Together they begin to understand the main conscious, as well as *unconscious*, aspects of the relationship between the two opposing large groups and the surrounding situation to be addressed.

During the psychopolitical dialogues under the direction of the psychoanalytically informed facilitating team—which consist of a series of multi-day meetings over several years—psychological obstacles against changing opposing large group's "pathological" ways of protecting large-group identity are brought to the surface, articulated, and understood by the participants. Fantasised threats to large-group identity, mostly due to reactivations of chosen traumas, are interpreted so that realistic communication can take place.

Psychopolitical dialogues are a series of intensive workshops during which the facilitating team brings into the open previously unrecognised thoughts and feelings, and helps the participants work through them. The goal is to prevent these disturbing thoughts and feelings from remaining in the shadows and interfering with a realistic evaluation of and relationship with the "enemy". In this sense, the workshops are therapeutic, but *not* at the level of personal problems. Since they deal with conflicts pertaining to participants' large-group identity, images of the enemy group, and historical grievances, they are primarily in the service of removing psychopolitical obstacles experienced by participants from opposing large groups.

During the dialogues the participants from the opposing large groups may suddenly experience a rapprochement. This closeness is then followed by a sudden withdrawal from one another—usually after focusing on minor differences between the opposing large groups, since such differences are perceived as the last protection of the psychological border between them. Then closeness is again experienced, followed by another withdrawal from one another—coming together and then pulling apart like an accordion. Denying and accepting derivatives of aggression within the participants towards the "enemy" large group, even when they are hidden, and attempts to protect large-group identities, underlie this behaviour. Effective discussion of real-world issues cannot take place unless one allows the "accordion playing" to continue for a while so that the swing in sentiments can be replaced by more secure feelings about participants' large-group identities.

Psychopolitical dialogues become a process where historical grievances, especially chosen traumas, are aired; perceptions, fears, and attitudes are articulated; and previously hidden psychological obstacles to reconciliation or change rise to the surface. Their aim is not to erase the images of past historical events and differences in large-group identity and culture, but rather to detoxify the relationship so that differences do not lead to renewed violence. When two large groups are in conflict, the enemy is obviously real, but it is also fantasised. If participants can differentiate their fantasised dangers from current issues, then negotiations and steps towards peace can become more realistic.

To be effective on a long-term basis, the series of psychopolitical workshops calls for the same thirty to forty influential participants (legislators, ambassadors, government officials, well-known scholars, or other public figures) to meet two to three times per year for three to four days each time. During the workshops there are plenary sessions, but most of the work is done in small groups led by members of the facilitating interdisciplinary team. The participants from the opposing large groups become spokespersons for their ethnic or national groups, and the facilitating team seeks to spread the insights gained to the broader population through concrete programmes that promote peaceful strategies and coexistence.

In order for the newly gained insights to have an impact on social and political policy, as well as on the populace at large, the final phase requires the collaborative development of concrete actions, programmes, and institutions. What is learned is operationalised so that more peaceful coexistence between large groups can be achieved and threats, especially the fantasised ones, to large-group identity coming from the Other can be tamed. The application of the Tree Model illustrates how psychoanalysts and (former) diplomats, as well as historians and persons from other disciplines can work together.

REFERENCES

Abraham, K. (1921). *Selected Papers of Karl Abraham*. London: Hogarth.

Achen, C. H., & Snidal, D. (1989). Rational deterrence theory and comparative case studies. *World Politics, 41*: 143–169.

Adams, M. V. (1996). *The Multicultural Imagination: "Race", Color, and the Unconscious*. London: Routledge.

Ainslie, R. C., & Solyom, A. E. (1986). The replacement of the fantastied oedipal child: A disruptive effect of sibling loss on the mother-infant relationship. *Psychoanalytic Psychology, 3*: 257–268.

Akhtar, S. (1999). *Immigration and Identity: Turmoil, Treatment, Transformation*. Northvale, NJ: Jason Aronson.

Alderdice, J. (2007). The individual, the group and the psychology of terrorism. *International Review of Psychiatry, 19*: 201–209.

Alderdice, J. (2010). Off the couch and round the conference table. In: A. Lemma & M. Patrick (Eds.), *Contemporary Psychoanalytic Applications* (pp. 15–32). London: Routledge.

Ali, T. (2001). Former USA policies allowed the Taliban to thrive. *Turkish Daily News*, Sept. 25, p. 16.

Allen, B. (1996). *Rape Warfare: The Hidden Genocide in Bosnia-Herzegovina and Croatia*. Minneapolis, MN: University of Minnesota Press.

Allison, G. T. (1971). *Essence of Decision: Explaining the Cuban Missile Crisis*. Boston: Little Brown.

Ambrose, S. E. (1989). *Nixon, Volume 2: The Triumph of a Politician 1962–1972.* New York: Simon and Schuster.

Anzieu, D. (1971). L'illusion groupale. *Nouvelle Revue de Psychanalyse, 4:* 73–93.

Anzieu, D. (1984). *The Group and the Unconscious.* London: Routledge & Kegan Paul.

Anzulovic, B. (1999). *Heavenly Serbia: From Myth to Genocide.* New York: New York University Press.

Apprey, M. (1993). The African-American experience: Transgenerational trauma and forced immigration. *Mind and Human Interaction, 4:* 70–75.

Apprey, M. (1998). Reinventing the self in the face of received transgenerational hatred in the African American community. *Mind and Human Interaction, 9:* 30–37.

Arlow, J. (1973). Motivations for peace. In: H. Z. Winnik, R. Moses, & M. Ostow (Eds.), *Psychological Basis of War* (pp. 193–204). Jerusalem: Jerusalem Academic Press.

Arnett, J. J. (2002). The psychology of globalization. *American Psychologist, 57:* 774–783.

Ascher, W., & Hirschfelder-Ascher, B. (2005). *Revitalizing Political Psychology: The Legacy of Harold D. Lasswell.* Mahwah, NJ: Lawrence Erlbaum.

Barner-Barry, C., & Rosenwein, R. (1985). *Psychological Perspectives on Politics.* Englewood Cliffs, NJ: Prentice-Hall.

Barston, R. P. (1988). *Modern Diplomacy.* London: Longman.

Berkes, N. (1964). *Türk Düşününde Batı Sorunu (The Western Question in Turkish Thought).* Ankara: Bilgi Yayınevi.

Bernard, V., Ottenberg, P., & Redl, F. (1973). Dehumanisation: A composite psychological defense in relation to modern war. In: N. Sanford & C. Comstock, (Eds.), *Sanctions for Evil: Sources of Social Destructiveness* (pp. 102–124). San Francisco: Jossey-Bass.

Bion, W. R. (1961). *Experiences in Groups.* London: Tavistock.

Bloom, P. (2010). *How Pleasure Works: The New Science of Why We Like What We Like.* New York: W. W. Norton.

Blos, P. (1979). *The Adolescent Passage: Developmental Issues.* New York: International Universities Press.

Böhm, T., & Kaplan, S. (2011). *Revenge: On the Dynamics of a Frightening Urge and its Taming.* London: Karnac.

Boyer, L. B. (1986). One man's need to have enemies: A psychoanalytic perspective. *Journal of Psychoanalytic Anthropology, 9:* 101–120.

Brenner, C. (1983). *The Mind in Conflict.* New York: International Universities Press.

Brenner, I. (1999). Returning to the fire: Surviving the Holocaust and "going back." *Journal of Applied Psychoanalytic Studies, 1:* 145–162.

Brenner, I. (2001). *Dissociation of Trauma: Theory, Phenomenology, and Technique*. Madison, CT: International Universities Press.

Brenner, I. (2004). *Psychic Trauma: Dynamics, Symptoms, and Treatment*. New York: Jason Aronson.

Brown, J. A. C. (1963). *Techniques of Persuasion: From Propaganda to Brainwashing*. Middlesex, England: Penguin.

Burns, J. M. (1984). *The Power to Lead: The Crisis of the American Presidency*. New York: Simon and Schuster.

Butler, T. (1993). Yugoslavia mon amour. *Mind and Human Interaction*, 4: 120–128.

Bytwerk, R. L. (2004). *Bending Spines: The Propagandas of Nazi Germany and the German Democratic Republic*. East Lansing: Michigan State University Press.

Cain, A. C., & Cain, B. S. (1964). On replacing a child. *Journal of the American Academy of Child Psychiatry*, 3: 443–456.

Campbell, R. (1983). An emotive place apart. *Art in America*, May, pp. 150–151.

Çevik, A. (2003). Globalization and identity. In: S. Varvin & V. D. Volkan (Eds.), *Violence or Dialogue: Psychoanalytic Insights to Terror and Terrorism* (pp. 91–98). London: International Psychoanalysis Library.

Chakotin, S. (1939). *The Rape of the Masses: The Psychology of Totalitarian Propaganda*. Middlesex, England: Penguin.

Chasseguet-Smirgel, J. (1984). *The Ego Ideal*. New York: W. W. Norton.

Chasseguet-Smirgel, J. (1996). Blood and nation. *Mind and Human Interaction*, 7: 31–36.

Chinard, G. (1979). *The Letters of Lafayette and Jefferson*. New York: Arno Press.

Cooper, A. M. (1989). Narcissism and masochism: The narcissistic-masochistic character. *Psychiatric Clinics of North America*, 12: 541–552.

Davidson, W. D., & Montville, J. V. (1981–1982). Foreign policy according to Freud. *Foreign Policy*, 45: 145–157.

Davis, D. (2000). The Pope who kidnapped a Jewish boy. *The Jerusalem Post*, March 24 (p. B4).

Eban, A. (1983). *The New Diplomacy: International Affairs in the Modern Age*. New York: Random House.

Elliott, M., Bishop, K., & Stokes, P. (2004). Societal PTSD? Historic shock in Northern Ireland. *Psychotherapy and Politics International*, 2: 1–16.

Emde, R. (1991). Positive emotions for psychoanalytic theory: Surprises from infancy research and new directions. *Journal of the American Psychoanalytic Association* (Supplement), 39: 5–44.

Emmert, T. A. (1990). *Serbian Golgotha: Kosovo, 1389*. New York: Columbia University Press.

Erikson, E. H. (1956). The problem of ego identity. *Journal of the American Psychoanalytic Association, 4*: 56–121.

Erikson, E. H. (1959). *Identity and the Life Cycle.* New York: International Universities Press.

Erikson, E. H. (1966). Ontogeny of ritualization. In: R. M. Lowenstein, L. M. Newman, M. Schur, & A. J. Solnit (Eds.), *Psychoanalysis: A General Psychology* (pp. 601–621). New York: International Universities Press.

Erikson, K. T. (1975). Loss of communality at Buffalo Creek. *American Journal of Psychiatry, 133*: 302–325.

Erlich, H. S. (1998). Adolescents' reactions to Rabin's assassination: A case of patricide? In: A. Esman (Ed.), *Adolescent Psychiatry: Developmental and Clinical Studies, 22* (pp. 189–205). London: The Analytic Press.

Erlich, H. S. (2010). A beam of darkness: Understanding the terrorist mind. In: H. Brunning & M. Perini (Eds.), *Psychoanalytic Perspectives on a Turbulent World* (pp. 3–15). London: Karnac.

Erlich, H. S. (2013). *The Couch in the Marketplace: Psychoanalysis and Social Reality.* London: Karnac.

Etzioni, A. (1967). Mixed scanning: A "third" approach to decision-making. *Public Administration Review, 27*: 385–392.

Faimberg, H. (2005). *The Telescoping of Generations: Listening to the Narcissistic Links Between Generations.* London: Routledge.

Fenichel, O. F. (1945). *The Psychoanalytic Theory of Neurosis.* New York: Norton.

Fornari, F. (1966). *The Psychoanalysis of War.* (Trans. A. Pfeifer). Bloomington: Indiana University Press, 1975.

Freud, A. (1936). The ego and the mechanisms of defense. In: *The Writings of Anna Freud, Volume 2.* New York: International Universities Press, 1966.

Freud, A., & Burlingham, D. (1942). *War and Children.* New York: International Universities Press.

Freud, S. (1905d). *Three Essays on the Theory of Sexuality. S.E., 7*: 130–243. London: Hogarth.

Freud, S. (1905e [1901]). *Fragment of an Analysis of a Case of Hysteria. S.E., 7*: 3–122. London: Hogarth.

Freud, S. (1917e). Mourning and melancholia. *S.E., 14*: 237–260. London: Hogarth.

Freud, S. (1918a). The taboo of virginity. *S.E., 11*: 191–208. London: Hogarth.

Freud, S. (1921c). *Group Psychology and the Analysis of the Ego. S.E., 18*: 67–143. London: Hogarth.

Freud, S. (1926d). Inhibitions, symptoms and anxiety. *S.E., 20*: 77–175. London: Hogarth.

Freud, S. (1930a). *Civilization and its Discontents. S.E.*, 21: 57–145. London: Hogarth.

Freud, S. (1933b). Why war? *S.E.*, 22: 197–215. London: Hogarth.

Fromm, M. G. (Ed.) (2012). *Lost in Transmission: Studies of Trauma Across Generations*. London: Karnac.

Furman, E. (1974). *A Child's Parent Dies: Studies in Childhood Bereavement*. New Haven, CT: Yale University Press.

George, A. L. (1969). The "operational code": A neglected approach to the study of political leaders and decision-making. *International Studies Quarterly*, 23: 190–222.

Glower, E. (1947). *War, Sadism and Pacifism: Further Essays on Group Psychology and War* London: Allen and Unwin.

Goenjian, A. K., Steinberg, A. M., Najarian, L. M., Fairbanks, L. A., Tashjian, M., & Pynoos, R. S. (2000). Prospective study of posttraumatic stress, anxiety, and depressive reactions after earthquake and political violence. *American Journal of Psychiatry*, 157: 911–916.

Goodall, J. (1986). *The Chimpanzees of Gombe: Patterns of Behavior*. Cambridge, MA: Harvard University Press.

Greenacre, P. (1969). The fetish and the transitional object. In: *Emotional Growth, Vol. 1* (pp. 315–334). New York: International Universities Press.

Grubrich-Simitis, I. (1979). Extremtraumatisierung als kumulatives trauma: Psychoanalytische studien über seelische nachwirkungen der konzentrationslagerhaft bei überlebenden und ihren kindern (Extreme traumatisation as a cumulative trauma: Psychoanalytic studies on the mental effects of imprisonment in concentration camps on survivors and their children). *Psyche*, 33: 991–1023.

Gutman, R. A. (1993). *A Witness to Genocide: The 1993 Pulitzer Prize-Winning Dispatches on the "Ethnic Cleansing" of Bosnia*. New York: Maxwell Macmillan International.

Hafez, M. M. (2006). *Manufacturing Human Bombs: The Making of Palestinian Suicide Bombers*. Washington, DC: United States Institute of Peace.

Halman, T. S. (1992). Istanbul. In: *The Last Lullaby* (pp. 8–9). Merrick, NY: Cross Cultural Communications.

Harris, M. (1992). Hidden transcripts in public places. *Mind and Human Interaction*, 3: 63–69.

Held, D. (1998). Democratization and globalization. In: A. Archibugi, D. Held, & M. Köhler (Eds.) *Re-imagining Political Community* (pp. 11–27). Stanford, CA: Stanford University Press.

Henry, M. (2000). Just an irritant. *The Jerusalem Post*, March 24 (p. B4).

Hersh, S. M. (1983). *The Price of Power: Kissinger in the Nixon White House*. Ontario, Canada: Summit Books.

Herzfeld, M. (1986). *Ours Once More: Folklore, Ideology, and the Making of Modern Greece*. New York: Pella.

Hitler, A. (1925–1926). *Mein Kampf (My Struggle)*. Boston: Houghton Mifflin, 1962.

Hollander, N. C. (1997). *Love in a Time of Hate: Liberation Psychology in Latin America*. New York: Other Press.

Hollander, N. (2010). *Uprooted Minds: Surviving the Political Terror in the Americas*. New York: Taylor and Francis.

Hopper, E. (2003). *Traumatic Experience in the Unconscious Life of Groups: The Fourth Basic Assumption: Incohesion: Aggregation/Massification or (ba) I:A/M*. London: Jessica Kingsley.

Horowitz, D. L. (1985). *Ethnic Groups in Conflict*. Berkeley: University of California Press.

Howell, W. N. (1993). Tragedy, trauma and triumph: Reclaiming integrity and initiative from victimization. *Mind and Human Interaction, 4*: 111–119.

Howell, W. N. (1995). "The evil that men do …": Societal effects of the Iraqi occupation of Kuwait. *Mind and Human Interaction, 6*: 150–169.

Itzkowitz, N. (1972). *Ottoman Empire and Islamic Tradition*. New York: Alfred A. Knopf.

Jacobson, E. (1964). *The Self and the Object World*. New York: International Universities Press.

Janis, I. L., & Mann, L. (1977). *Decision-making: A Psychological Analysis of Conflict, Choice, and Commitment*. New York: Free Press.

Jervis, R., Lebow, N., & Stein, J. G. (1985). *Psychology of Deterrence*. Baltimore, MD: John Hopkins.

Jowett, G. S., & O'Donnell, V. (1992). *Propaganda and Persuasion*. New York: Sage.

Kakar, S. (1996). *The Colors of Violence: Cultural Identities, Religion, and Conflict*. Chicago: University of Chicago Press.

Kaplan, R. D. (1993). *Balkan Ghosts: A Journey Through History*. New York: Vintage.

Keinon, H. (2000). Ring around the Rabbi. *The Jerusalem Post*, March 31 (p. B4).

Kernberg, O. F. (1970). A psychoanalytic classification of character pathology. *Journal of the American Psychoanalytic Association, 18*: 800–822.

Kernberg, O. F. (1975). *Borderline Conditions and Pathological Narcissism*. New York: Jason Aronson.

Kernberg, O. F. (1976). *Object Relations Theory and Clinical Psychoanalysis*. New York: Jason Aronson.

Kernberg, O. F. (1980). *Internal World and External Reality: Object Relations Theory Applied*. New York: Jason Aronson.

Kernberg, O. F. (1989). Mass psychology through the analytic lens. Paper presented at *Through the Looking Glass: Freud's Impact on Contemporary Culture meeting*, Philadelphia, PA, September 23 (unpublished).

Kernberg, O. F. (2010). Some observations on the process of mourning. *International Journal of Psychoanalysis, 91*: 601–619.

Kertzer, D. (1997). *The Kidnapping of Edgardo Mortara*. New York: Knopf.

Kestenberg, J. S. (1982). A psychological assessment based on analysis of a survivor's child. In: M. S. Bergman & M. E. Jucovy (Eds.), *Generations of the Holocaust* (pp. 158–177). New York: Columbia University Press.

Kestenberg, J. S., & Brenner, I. (1996). *The Last Witness: The Child Survivor of the Holocaust*. Washington, DC: American Psychiatric Press.

Khrushchev, N. S. (1970). *Khrushchev Remembers*. Boston, MA: Little, Brown.

Kinnvall, C. (2004). Globalization and religious nationalism: Self, identity, and the search for ontological security. *Political Psychology, 25*: 741–767.

Kinross, Lord (1965). *Atatürk: A Biography of Mustafa Kemal, Father of modern Turkey*. New York: William Morrow.

Kissinger, H. A. (1979). *White House Years*. Boston: Little, Brown.

Kitromilides, P. M. (1990). "Imagined communities" and the origins of the national question in the Balkans. In: M. Blickhorn & T. Veremis (Eds.), *Modern Greek Nationalism and Nationality* (pp. 23–65). Athens: Sage-Eliamep.

Klein, D. (1985). Deductive economic methodology in the French Enlightenment: Cadillac and Desutt de Tracy. *History of Political Economy, 17*: 51–71.

Klein, M. (1946). Notes on some schizoid mechanisms. *International Journal of Psychoanalysis, 27*: 99–110.

Kogan, I. (1995). *The Cry of Mute Children: A Psychoanalytic Perspective of the Second Generation of the Holocaust*. London: Free Association.

Kohut, H. (1966). Forms and transformations of narcissism. *Journal of the American Psychoanalytic Association, 14*: 243–272.

Kohut, H. (1971). *The Analysis of the Self: A Systematic Approach to the Psychoanalytic Treatment of Narcissistic Personality Disorder*. New York: International Universities Press.

Kohut, H. (1977). *The Restoration of the Self*. New York: International Universities Press.

Kriegman, G. (1988). Entitlement attitudes: Psychological and therapeutic implications. In: V. D. Volkan & T. C. Rodgers (Eds.), *Attitudes of Entitlement: Theoretical and Clinical Issues* (pp. 1–21). Charlottesville: University Press of Virginia.

Kris, E. (1943). Some problems of war propaganda: A note on propaganda new and old. *Psychoanalytic Quarterly, 12*: 381–399.

Kris, E. (1944). *German Radio Propaganda: Report on Home Broadcasts during the War*. New York: Oxford University Press.

Kris, E. (1952). *Psychoanalytic Explorations in Art*. New York: International Universities Press.

Kris, E. (1975). *Selected Papers of Ernst Kris*. New Haven: Yale University Press.

Krystal, H. (Ed.) (1968). *Massive Psychic Trauma*. New York: International Universities Press.

Lasswell, H. D. (1932). The triple-appeal principle: A contribution of psychoanalysis to political and social science. *American Journal of Sociology*, 37: 523–538.

Lasswell, H. D. (1936). *Politics: Who Gets What, When, How*. New York: Meridian.

Lasswell, H. D. (1938). Foreword. In: G. G. Bruntz (Ed.), *Allied Propaganda and the Collapse of the German Empire in 1918* (pp. v–viii). Stanford, CA: Stanford University Press.

Lasswell, H. D. (1948). *The Analysis of Political Behavior: An Empirical Approach*. London: Routledge & Kegan Paul.

Lasswell, H. D. (1963). *The Future of Political Science*. New York: Atherton.

Laub, D., & Auerhahn, N. C. (1993). Knowing and not knowing massive psychic trauma: Forms of traumatic memory. *International Journal of Psychoanalysis*, 74: 287–302.

Laub, D., & Podell, D. (1997). Psychoanalytic listening to historical trauma: The conflict of knowing and the imperative act. *Mind and Human Interaction*, 8: 245–260.

Le Bon, G. (1895). *The Crowd: A Study of the Popular Mind*. London: T. F. Unwin, 1897.

Le Bon, G. (1910). *La Psychologie Politigue, et la Défense Sociale*. Paris: Flammarion.

Lehtonen, J. (2003). The dream between neuroscience and psychoanalysis: Has feeding an impact on brain function and the capacity to create dream images in infants? *Psychoanalysis in Europe Bulletin*, 57: 175–182.

Levin, S. (1970). On psychoanalysis of attitudes of entitlement. *Bulletin of the Philadelphia Association of Psychoanalysis*, 20: 1–10.

Lewis, B. (2000). Propaganda in the Middle East. Paper presented at the International Conference in Commemoration of the 78th Birthday of Yitzhak Rabin: "*Patterns of Political Discourse: Propaganda, Incitement and Freedom of Speech,*" February 29 (unpublished).

Lifton, R. J. (1968). *Death in Life: Survivors of Hiroshima*. New York: Random House.

Lifton, R. J. (1989). *Thought Reform and the Psychology of Totalism: A Study of "Brainwashing" in China*. Chapel Hill: University of North Carolina Press.

Lifton, R. J., & Olson, E. (1976). The human meaning of total disaster: The Buffalo Creek experience. *Psychiatry, 39*: 1–18.

Liu, J. H., & Mills, D. (2006). Modern racism and neo-liberal globalization: The discourses of plausible deniability and their multiple functions. *Journal of Community and Applied Social Psychology, 16*: 83–99.

Loewenberg, P. (1991). Uses of anxiety. *Partisan Review, 3*: 514–525.

Loewenberg, P. (1995). *Fantasy and Reality in History.* New York: Oxford University Press.

Mahler, M. S., & Furer, M. (1968). *On Human Symbiosis and the Vicissitudes of Individuation.* New York: International Universities Press.

Markides, K. C. (1977). *The Rise and Fall of the Cyprus Republic.* New Haven: Yale University Press.

Markovic, M. S. (1983). The secret of Kosovo. (Trans. C. Kramer). In: V. D. Mihailovich (Ed.), *Landmarks in Serbian Culture and History* (pp. 111–131). Pittsburg, PA: Serb National Foundation.

Mazo, E., & Hess, E. (1967). *Nixon: A Political Portrait.* New York: Popular Library.

Mitani, J. C., Watts, D. P., & Amsler, S. J. (2010). Lethal intergroup aggression leads to territorial expansion in wild chimpanzees. *Current Biology, 20*: R507–R508.

Mitscherlich, A. (1971). Psychoanalysis and the aggression of large groups. *International Journal of Psychoanalysis, 52*: 161–167.

Mitscherlich, A., & Mitscherlich, M. (1975). *The Inability to Mourn: Principals of Collective Behavior.* (Trans. B. R. Placzek). New York: Grove.

Money-Kyrle, R. E. (1941). The psychology of propaganda. *British Journal of Medical Psychology, 19*: 82–94.

Morton, T. L. (2005). Prejudice in an era of economic globalization and international interdependence. In: J. L. Chin (Ed.), *The Psychology of Prejudice and Discrimination: Disability, Religion, Physique, and Other Traits, Volume 4* (pp. 135–160). Westport, CT: Praeger.

Moses, R. (1982). The group-self and the Arab-Israeli Conflict. *International Review of Psychoanalysis, 9*: 55–65.

Moses-Hrushovski, R. (2000). *Grief and Grievance: The Assassination of Yitzhak Rabin.* London: Minerva.

Motolinia, T. (1951). *History of Indians of New Spain.* (Trans. F. B. Steck). Washington, DC: Academy of American Franciscan History.

Murphy, R. F. (1957). Intergroup hostility and social cohesion. *American Anthropologist, 59*: 1018–1035.

Narváez, L., & Díaz, J. (2010). The general principles of forgiveness and reconciliation. In: L. Narváez, L. E Soares, D. Hicks, S. Abadian, R. Peterson, J. Diaz, & P. Monroy (Eds.), *Political Culture of Forgiveness and Reconciliation* (pp. 171–220). Bogota, Colombia: Fundación para la Reconcilatión.

Niederland, W. G. (1961). The problem of the survivor. *Journal of the Hillside Hospital, 10*: 233–247.

Niederland, W. G. (1968). Clinical observations on the "survivor syndrome." *International Journal of Psychoanalysis, 49*: 313–315.

Nixon, R. (1978). *RN: The Memoirs of Richard Nixon*. New York: Grosset and Dunlap.

Ochsner, J. K. (1997). A space of loss: The Vietnam Veterans Memorial. *Journal of Architectural Education, 50*: 156–171.

Pinson, M. (Ed.) (1994). *The Muslims of Bosnia-Herzegovina*. Cambridge, MA: Harvard University Press.

Politis, N. G. (1872). Khelidhonisma (Swallow song). *Neoelinika Analekta, 1*: 354–368.

Politis, N. G. (1882). *Introductory Lecture for the Class in Hellenic Mythology* (In Greek). Athens: Aion.

Pollock, G. H. (1989). *The Mourning-Liberation Process, Volumes 1 and 2*. Madison, CT: International Universities Press.

Rangell, L. (1980). *The Mind of Watergate*. New York: Norton.

Rashid, A. (2000). *Taliban: Islam, Oil and the New Great Game in Central Asia*. London: I. B. Tauris.

Ratliff, J. M. (2004). The persistence of national differences in a globalizing world: The Japanese struggle for competitiveness in advanced information technologies. *Journal of Socio-Economics, 33*: 71–88.

Raviv, A., Sadeh, A., Raviv, A., Silberstein, O., & Diver, O. (2000). Young Israelis' reactions to national trauma: The Rabin assassination and terror attacks. *Political Psychology, 21*: 299–322.

Roland, A. (2011). *Asians and Asian Americans in a Global Era*. New York: Oxford University Press.

Saathoff, G. (1995). In the hall of mirrors: One Kuwaiti's captive memories. *Mind and Human Interaction, 6*: 170–178.

Saathoff, G. B. (1996). Kuwait's children: Identity in the shadow of the storm. *Mind and Human Interaction, 7*: 181–91.

Saunders, H. (1990). An historic challenge to rethink how nation states relate. In: V. D. Volkan, D. A. Julius, & J. V. Montville (Eds.), *The Psychodynamics of International Relationships, Volume I: Concepts and Theories* (pp. 1–30). Lexington, MA: Lexington Books.

Schwoebel, R. (1967). *The Shadows of the Crescent: The Renaissance Image of the Turk (1453–1517)*. New York: St. Martin's Press.

Scruton, R. (1982). *A Dictionary of Political Thought*. New York: Harper and Row.

Šebek, M. (1992). Anality in the totalitarian system and the psychology of post-totalitarian society. *Mind and Human Interaction, 4*: 52–59.

Šebek, M. (1994). Psychopathology of everyday life in the post-totalitarian society. *Mind and Human Interaction, 5*: 104–109.

Seib, P. M. (1996). *Headline Diplomacy: How News Coverage Affects Foreign Policy.* New York: Praeger/Greenwood.

Sells, M. A. (2002). The construction of Islam in Serbian religious mythology and its consequences. In: M. Shatzmiller (Ed.), *Islam and Bosnia* (pp. 56–85). Montreal: McGill-Queen's University Press.

Smith, D. L. (2011). *Less Than Human: Why We Demean, Enslave and Exterminate Others.* New York: St. Martin's Press.

Smith, J. (2000). The father, the son and the holy see. *The Washington Post,* June 23 (pp. A1, A27).

Smith, J. H. (1975). On the work of mourning. In: B. Schoenberg, I. Gerber, A. Wiener, A. H. Kutscher, D. Peretz, & A. C. Carr (Eds.), *Bereavement: Its Psychological Aspects* (pp. 18–25). New York: Columbia University Press.

Stein, H. F. (1990). The international and group milieu of ethnicity: Identifying generic group dynamic issues. *Canadian Review of Studies in Nationalism, 17*: 107–130.

Steinberg, B. (1996). *Shame and Humiliation: Presidential Decision-making on Vietnam: A Psychoanalytic Interpretation.* Montreal: McGill-Queen's University Press.

Stiglitz, J. E. (2003). *Globalisation and its Discontents.* New York: W. W. Norton.

Spitz, R. (1965). *The First Year of Life.* New York: International Universities Press.

Stern, D. N. (1985). *The Interpersonal World of the Infant: A View from Psychoanalysis and Developmental Psychology.* New York: Basic.

Stern, J. (2001). Deviance in the Nazi society. *Mind and Human Interaction, 12*: 218–237.

Swift, E. M. (1995). Book to the future. *Sports Illustrated,* July 3, p. 32.

Tähkä, V. (1984). Dealing with object loss. *Scandinavian Psychoanalytic Review, 7*: 13–33.

Tate, C. (1996). Freud and his "Negro": Psychoanalysis as ally and enemy of African Americans. *Journal for the Psychoanalysis of Culture and Society, 1*: 53–62.

Thompson, K. W. (1980). *Masters of International Thought.* Baton Rouge: Louisiana State University Press.

Tucker, R. C. (1973). *Stalin as Revolutionary.* New York: Norton.

Varvin, S., & Volkan, V. D. (Eds.). (2003). *Violence or Dialogue: Psychoanalytic Insights on Terror and Terrorism.* London: International Psychoanalytical Association.

Vasquez, J. A. (1986). Morality and politics. In: J. A. Vasquez (Ed.), *Classics of International Relations* (pp. 1–8). Englewood Cliffs, NJ: Prentice-Hall.

Volkan, K. (1992). The Vietnam War Memorial. *Mind and Human Interaction*, 3: 73–77.

Volkan, V. D. (1972). The linking objects of pathological mourners. *Archives of General Psychiatry*, 27: 215–221.

Volkan, V. D. (1976). *Primitive Internalized Object Relations: A Clinical Study of Schizophrenic, Borderline and Narcissistic Patients*. New York: International Universities Press.

Volkan, V. D. (1979a). *Cyprus—War and Adaptation: A Psychoanalytic History of Two Ethnic Groups in Conflict*. Charlottesville: University Press of Virginia.

Volkan, V. D. (1979b). The glass bubble of a narcissistic patient. In: J. LeBoit & A. Capponi (Eds.), *Advances in Psychotherapy of the Borderline Patient* (pp. 405–431). New York: Jason Aronson.

Volkan, V. D. (1981). *Linking Objects and Linking Phenomena: A Study of the Forms, Symptoms, Metapsychology, and Therapy of Complicated Mourning*. New York: International Universities Press.

Volkan, V. D. (1988). *The Need to Have Enemies and Allies: From Clinical Practice to International Relationships*. Northvale, NJ: Jason Aronson.

Volkan, V. D. (1997). *Bloodlines: From Ethnic Pride to Ethnic Terrorism*. New York: Farrar, Straus and Giroux.

Volkan, V. D. (2004). *Blind Trust: Large Groups and Their Leaders in Times of Crisis and Terror*. Charlottesville, VA: Pitchstone.

Volkan, V. D. (2006a). *Killing in the Name of Identity: A Study of Bloody Conflicts*. Charlottesville, VA: Pitchstone.

Volkan, V. D. (2006b). What some monuments tell us about mourning and forgiveness. In: E. Barkin & A. Karn (Eds.), *Taking Wrongs Seriously: Apologies and Reconciliation* (pp. 115–131). Stanford, CA: Stanford University Press.

Volkan, V. D. (2007a). Individuals and societies as "perennial mourners": Their linking objects and public memorials. In: B. Wilcock, L. C. Bohm, & R. Curtis (Eds.), *On Death and Dying: Psychoanalysts' Reflections on Finality, Transformations and New Beginnings* (pp. 42–59). Philadelphia: Routledge.

Volkan, V. D. (2007b). Not letting go: From individual perennial mourners to societies with entitlement ideologies. In: L. G. Fiorini, S. Lewkowicz, & T. Bokanowsi (Eds.), *On Freud's "Mourning and Melancholia"* (pp. 90–109). London: International Psychoanalytic Association.

Volkan, V. D. (2010). *Psychoanalytic Technique Expanded: A Textbook on Psychoanalytic Treatment*. Istanbul: Oa.

Volkan, V. D. (2011). Play and tract two diplomacy. In: M. C. Akhtar & M. Nayer (Eds.), *Play and Playfulness: Developmental, Clinical, and Socio-Cultural Aspects* (pp. 150–171). New York: Jason Aronson.

Volkan, V. D. (2013). *Enemies on the Couch: A Psychopolitical Journey through War and Peace.* Durham, NC: Pitchstone.

Volkan, V. D. (2014). *Animal Killer: Transmission of War Trauma from One Generation to the Next.* London: Karnac.

Volkan, V. D., & Ast, G. (1997). *Siblings in the Unconscious and Psychopathology.* Madison, CT: International Universities Press.

Volkan, V. D., & Fowler, J. C. (2009). Large-group narcissism and political leaders with narcissistic personality organization. *Psychiatric Annals, 39*: 214–222.

Volkan, V. D., & Itzkowitz, N. (1984). *The Immortal Atatürk: A Psychobiography.* Chicago: Chicago University Press.

Volkan, V. D., & Itzkowitz, N. (1993). "Istanbul, not Constantinople": The Western world's view of "the Turk". *Mind and Human Interaction, 4*: 129–140.

Volkan, V. D., & Itzkowitz, N. (1994). *Turks and Greeks: Neighbours in Conflict.* Cambridgeshire, England: Eothen Press.

Volkan, V. D., & Kayatekin, S. (2006). Extreme religious fundamentalism and violence: Some psychoanalytic and psychopolitical thoughts. *Psyche & Geloof, 17*: 71–91.

Volkan, V. D., & Zintl, E. (1993). *Life After Loss: The Lessons of Grief.* New York: Charles Scribner's Sons.

Volkan, V. D., Ast, G., & Greer, W. (2002). *The Third Reich in the Unconscious: Transgenerational Transmission and its Consequences.* New York: Brunner-Routledge.

Volkan, V. D., Itzkowitz, N., & Dod, A. (1997). *Richard Nixon: A Psychobiography.* New York: Columbia University Press.

von Rochau, A. L. (1853). *Grundsätze der Realpolitik.* Frankfurt: Ullstein, 1972.

Vulliamy, E. (1994). *Seasons in Hell: Understanding Bosnia's War.* New York: St. Martin's Press.

Waelder, R. (1930). The principle of multiple function: Observations on over-determination. *Psychoanalytic Quarterly, 5*: 45–62, 1936.

Waelder, R. (1971). Psychoanalysis and history. In: B. B. Wolman (Ed.), *The Psychoanalytic Interpretation of History* (pp. 3–22). New York: Basic.

Weber, M. (1923). *Wirtschaft und Gessellschaft, 2 volumes.* Tübingen: J. C. B. Mohr.

Weigert, E. (1967). Narcissism: Benign and malignant forms. In: R. W. Gibson (Ed.), *Crosscurrents in Psychiatry and Psychoanalysis* (pp. 222–238). Philadelphia: Lippincott.

Williams, R. M., & Parkes, C. M. (1975). Psychosocial effects of disaster: Birth rate in Aberfan. *British Medical Journal, 2*: 303–304.

Wills, G. (2000). *Papal Sin: Structures of Deceit*. New York: Doubleday.

Winnicott, D. W. (1953). Transitional objects and transitional phenomena. *International Journal of Psychoanalysis, 34*: 89–97.

Wolfenstein, M. (1966). How is mourning possible? *Psychoanalytic Study of the Child, 21*: 93–123.

Wolfenstein, M., & Kliman, G. (Eds.), (1965). *Children and the Death of a President: Multi-disciplinary Studies*. Garden City, NY: Doubleday.

Worthington, E. (2001). *Five Steps to Forgiveness*. New York: Crown.

Worthington, E. (2005). *Handbook of Forgiveness*. New York: Taylor & Francis.

Young, K. (1969). *The Greek Passion: A Study in People and Politics*. London: J. M. Dent.

Zamblios, S. (1856). Some philosophical researches on the modern Greek language (In Greek). *Pandora, 7*: 369–380, 484–489.

Zamblios, S. (1859). *Whence the Vulgar Word Traghoudho? Thoughts Concerning Hellenic Poetry* (in Greek). Athens: P. Soutsas & A. Ktenas.

INDEX

Abkhazia 58
Abraham, K. 78
Achen, C. H. 2
Adams, M. V. 5
adolescent passage 21, 54
aggression ix, xiv, 6, 28, 50–51, 60–62,
    68, 83, 97, 100, 126
Ainslie, R C. 22
Akhtar, S. 18
Albania xii, xviii, 4, 63
Albanians 63, 95
Alderdice, Lord xviii, 5
Ali, T. 118
Allen, B. 101
Allison, G. T. 2
Alp Arslan, Sultan 39
Ambrose, S. E. 87–88
American Psychiatric
    Association 3
        Committee on Psychiatry and
            Foreign Affairs xvii

American Psychoanalytic
    Association 5
Amsler, S. J. 28
Anzieu, D. 7
Anzulovic, B. 99
Apprey, M. 5
Aquinas, T. 12
Arabs xv, xvii, 3, 5, 9, 18, 41, 62
Arafat, Y. xviii, 106–107
Arlow, J. 9
Armenians 30, 47
Arnett, J. J. 123
Ascher, W. 124
Assad, H. 107
Ast, G. 4, 22, 74, 96
Atatürk, K. 33, 61
Atta, M. 118
Auerhahn, N. C. 22
Austro-Hungarian Empire 93–94
Aygün, H. 99
Azerbaijanis 30, 47

Baltic Republics 4
Barak, E. 104, 106–108
Barner-Barry, C. 2
Barston, R. P. 121
Bataan Death March 22
Battle of Badr 117
Battle of Bilá Hora 24
Battle of Constantinople 41
Battle of Culloden 24
Battle of Kosovo 24, 89–92, 98
Battle of Manzigert 39
Bayezid, Sultan 90
Berkes, N. 41
Bernard, V. 49, 61
Bion, W. R. xi, 9
biosocial degeneration 48
biosocial regeneration 48
Bishop, K. 5
blind trust xv
Bloom , P. 19
Blos, P. 21, 54, 67
Böhm, T. 5
Bonnie Prince Charlie 24, 27
borders 49, 62
    psychological 14, 30, 49, 62, 123
Bosnia xii, 93–95, 99–101
Bosnians xviii, 21, 56, 93–94, 98–101
Boyer, L. B. 28–29
brainwashing 113
Brenner, C. 12
Brenner, I. 4, 22
Brown, J. A. C. 112
Burlingham, D. 57
Burns, J. M. 79
Bush, G. W. 41
Butler, T. 99–100
Bytwerk, R. L. 113

Cain, A. C. 22
Cain, B. S. 22
Calvin, J. 33
Cambodia 86–88

Campbell, R. 75
Carter, J. xviii, 100
Center for the Study of Mind and
    Human Interaction (CSMHI) xii,
    xvii, 4, 51, 55, 72–73, 122, 125
Çevik, A. xviii, 123
Chakotin, S. 110
change of function 24
Chanturia, G. 46
Chasseguet-Smirgel, J. 7, 121–122
China 85
chosen glories xiv, 25, 31, 61–62, 99
chosen traumas xiv, 15, 24–25, 31, 35,
    39, 43, 61–63, 71, 103, 125–126
Clinton, B. 104, 106–108
Cooper, A. M. 84
Covington, C. xviii
Croatia xii, 4, 89, 93–95
Croats xiii, 63, 81, 94–95
Crusades 12, 39, 41
Cyprus 3, 26–27, 42–43, 48–49, 55
Czechs 24

Davidson, W. 15
Davis, D. 105
death instinct x
dehumanisation xv, 23, 29, 49, 61, 112
demonisation xv, 80
depositing 21–23, 27
devşirme 92
Díaz, J. 124
dissenters 21, 30
Diver, O. 46
Dod, A. 85–86

Eban, A. 122
Ecevit, B. 3
Egypt xii, 62, 118
Egyptians xvii, 2–3
Einstein, A. xi–x, 9–10
Elliot, M. 5
Emde, R. 19

Emmert, T. A. 90, 94
entitlement xii, 35–36, 42, 50, 56, 81, 98
entitlement ideologies 31, 35, 39–40, 43–44, 71, 110
    American exceptionalism 37
    Christoslavism 37, 101
    irredentism 36
    Megali Idea 36, 39, 42–43
    Pan-Turanism 36
Enver Hoxha xviii, 63
Erikson, E. 18–20, 28, 61
Erikson, K. 47
Erlich, H. S. 5, 10, 46, 118
Estonia xii
Estonians xiii, 25
ethnic cleansing xiii, 99
Etzioni, A. 2
externalisation 7, 13, 23, 49, 59, 63, 100, 103
    targets of 25–27

Fabri, F. 40
Faimberg, H. 22
Fenichel, O. F. 68
Filelfo, G. M. 40–41
Finnish 27
forgiveness xv, 64, 71, 124
Fornari, F. 4
Fowler, J. C. 83
Franz Ferdinand, Archduke 94
Freud, A. 54, 57
Freud, S. x–xi, 1–2, 4, 6–7, 9–10, 14, 18, 60, 62, 65–66, 68, 78, 82–83, 111
Friedman, R. xviii
Fromm, G. xviii, 5
Furer, M. 19, 117
Furman, E. 66

Gavrilo Princip 94, 119
Gaza 115

George, A. L. 2
George IV, King 27
Georgia xii, xviii, 4, 20, 46, 50, 55, 58, 72
Georgian xiii, 20, 50, 58, 72–74
Germans 25, 62, 112
Germany xviii, 4, 8, 112–113, 122
glass bubble fantasy 84–85, 87
globalisation 15, 123
Glower, E. 4, 113
Goebbels, J. 112, 114
Goenjian, A. K. 47
Goodall, J. 28
Gorbachev, M. xviii, 95
Gourguechon, P. 5
Grabert, H. 96
grandiose self 83–84, 88
Greece xii, 3, 42–43, 47
Greeks xiii, 24, 26, 36, 42, 46, 110
    Cypriot Greeks 43, 48–49
Greenacre, P. 70
Greer, W. 4, 22, 74, 113
Grubrich-Simitis, I. 4
Gül, A. xviii
Gutman, R. A. 100, 110

Hafez, M. M. 115–116
Halman, T. 42
Hariri, R. 46
Harris, M. 41
Held, D. 123
Henry, M. 105
Hersh, S. M. 87
Herzfeld, M. 42
Hess, E. 85
Hirschfelder-Ascher, B. 124
Hitler, A. 34, 112, 114
Hollander, N. 5, 37
Holocaust xix, 4, 22, 25, 74
Hopper, E. 60
Horowitz, D. L. 63
Howell, W. N. 51

humiliation xii, 5, 23, 29, 35, 40–41, 53, 55–57, 81, 85–86, 91, 93–95, 98, 112, 116
Hungarian 21
hungry self 84, 88
Hussein, S. 6, 51, 53, 61–62

identification 6, 20–21, 23, 27–28, 54, 56, 65, 67–68, 94, 115
    with aggressor 10, 54, 116
identity 22, 28–29, 78
    individual xiii, 14, 18–25, 29–30, 49, 83–84, 115
    large-group xiii–xvi, 8–14, 18, 20–31, 44–50, 55, 59–63, 80, 90, 97, 102–103, 108, 112, 117
    markers 20–21, 24, 60, 126
India 5, 20, 63
internalisation 59, 63
International Dialogue Initiative (IDI) xviii
International Institute of Intellectual Co-operation xi
International Negotiation Network (INN) xviii
International Psychoanalytic Association (IPA) 5
    Terror and Terrorism Study Group 5
introject 68
introjection 59, 63
Iran xviii, 113
Iraq 6, 62
Iraqis xviii, 51–53, 55, 61, 63, 67
Israel xii, xvii–xviii, 2, 46, 104–108, 113
Israelis xv, 3, 9, 46, 104–108
Itzkowitz, N. 3, 21, 26–27, 33–35, 39, 41, 61, 85–86, 92, 122

Jacobson, E. 83
Janis, I. L. 2–3

Jervis, R. 2
John Paul II, Pope 104–106
Jowett, G. S. 111

Kaczyński, L. 24
Kaczyńska, M. 24
Kakar, S. 5, 20
Kaplan, R. D. 95, 98
Kaplan, S. 5
Karadžic, R. 100
Katyn Forest massacre 24
Kayatekin, S. 123
Keinon, H. 106
Kemalism 34–35
Kennedy, J. F. 45
Kernberg, O. F. 7, 65, 70, 83–85
Kertzer, D. 105
Kestenberg, J. S. 4, 22
Khomeini, Ayatollah 113
Khrushchev, N. S. 82
King, M. L. 45
Kinnvall, C. 123
Kinross, Lord 92
Kissinger, H. A. 86–88
Kitromilides, P. M. 42
Klein, D. 33
Klein, M. 22
Kliman, G. 45
Kogan, I. 4, 22
Kohut, H. 83
Kriegman, G. 36
Kris, E. 4, 13, 19–20, 113–114
Krystal, H. 4
Kurds 62
Kuwaitis 51–55

large-group progression 58, 64
large-group regression xiv, 58–61, 63, 80
Lasswell, H. D. 4, 111–112, 124
Latvia xii, 64
Laub, D. 4, 22

Lazar Hrebeljanović, Prince 90–91, 93–95, 97–100
leaders xiv, xv, xvi, 6–7, 14, 24, 61
   leaders–followers xviii, xix, 8, 79
   transactional 78–79, 81
   transforming 78–79, 81
Lebanon xviii, 46
Le Bon, G. 111, 114
Lebow, N. 2
Lehtonen, J. 19
Levin , S. 36
Levine, H. B. xi–xvi
Lewis, B. 111
Lifton, R. J. 46, 48, 113
linking objects 69–71, 74
linking phenomena 69–70
Lithuania xii
Liu, J. H. 123
Loewenberg, P. 5, 13, 35

magical thinking xiv, 63–64, 124
Mahfouz, A. 5
Mahler, M. 19,117
Mandela, N. 79–81
Mann, L. 2–3
Markides, K. C. 42
Markovic, M. S. 90, 92–93
Marx, K. 114
Marxism 33–34
masochism xv, 9, 31
Mazo, E. 85
McAuliffe, C. 46
Mehmed II, Sultan 40–41
memorials 53, 71, 74–75
   Crying Father 72–73
   Kosovo Memorial 98
   Vietnam Veterans Memorial 74–75
   Yad Vashem 74
Mesmer, A. 111
migrations 15, 21, 49
Miladić, R. 100

Mills, D. 123
Miloševic, S. 80–81, 88, 95–99, 101, 110
Miloš Kobila 91, 93–94
Milutinović, M. 110
minor differences 14, 62–63, 126
Mirjana Marković 96
Mitani, J. C. 28
Mitscherlich, A. 4, 24
Mitscherlich, M. 4, 24
Money-Kyrle, R. E. 4, 113
Montifiore, M. 105
Montville, J. V. 15
morality 12–13, 64
Mortara family 105
Morton, T. L. 123
Moses, R. 5
Moses-Hrushovski, R. 46
Motolinia, T. 41
mourning xii, xv, 7–8, 23, 29, 36, 40, 50, 57, 65–76, 92, 97–98, 124
Muhammad, Prophet 114
Murad I, Sultan 90, 92
Murphy, R. F. 29
Mussolini, B. 114

Napoleon III 105
narcissism 9, 28, 83, 85
   individual 85, 116
   large-group 8–9, 109, 116, 124
      malignant 8
      masochistic 8
   of minor differences 62
narcissistic investment 8, 21, 23, 36, 49, 55, 60, 103
narcissistic personality 83–85, 87, 96–97, 109
Narváez, L. 124
Nazi 5, 8, 29, 34, 57, 94, 96, 105, 112–114
Nebuchadnezzar II 25
Neu, J. 100

Nicholas V, Pope 40
Niederland, W. 4
Nietzsche, F. 114
Nixon, R. 85–88
Northern Ireland 5
Northern Irish Catholics 30
Northern Irish Protestants 30
North Korea 7

Ochberg, F. xviii
Ochsner, J. K. 71, 74
Olson, E. 46
Osama bin Laden 118, 122
Ottenberg, P. 49, 61
Ottomans 21, 24, 37, 40–42, 61, 90–94,
    97, 99–100, 110–111, 113, 117

Palestine xii
Palestinians xviii, 3, 107–108, 116–118
Panama 12
Parkes, C. M. 47
Pender, V. 5
Permanent Committee for Literature
    and the Arts of the League of
    Nations xi
Peru 5
Philippines 22
Piccolomini, A. S. 40
Pinson, M. 21
Pius IX, Pope 105
projection 13, 23, 49, 59, 63, 100, 103
projective identification 22
propaganda xiv, 4, 6–7, 59, 63–64, 79,
    96–97, 99–100, 107–119
Podell, D. 4
Polish 24
Politis, N. G. 42
Pollock, G. H. 66
post-traumatic stress disorder
    (PTSD) 47
prejudice 5, 10–11, 15, 17–18, 21, 23,
    25–26, 28–31, 36, 60, 64

pseudo species 28–29
psychic reality 58, 64, 112
purification 63–64, 81, 110, 112

Rabin, Y. 45, 108
racism xiii, 10, 18, 113, 121, 123
    neo- 17
Rangel, L. 64, 83
Rashid, A. 117
Ratliff, J. M. 123
Raviv, A. 46
Realpolitik xi, 1, 15, 43, 87
Redl, F. 49, 61
religious fundamentalism xiii, 31, 40,
    63, 79, 81, 99–100, 113–114, 118,
    122
replacement child 22
Riefenstahl, L. 112
Robespierre, M. 114
Roland, A. 5
Romanians 21, 94
Rosenwein, R. 2
Rubinstein, E. 106
Russia, xii–xiii, 106
Russians xiii, 24–25, 31, 50, 64, 99
Rüütel, A. xviii
Rwanda 29

Saathoff, G. 51, 53
Sadat, A. xv–xvii, 2
Sadeh, A. 46
sadism xv, 8–9, 31
Saladin, Sultan 61–62
Sarid, Y. 106
Saunders, H. 122
Scholz, R. xviii
Schwoebel, R. 40–41
Scotland 27
Scruton, R. 33–34
Šebek, M. 5
second individuation 54
Seib, P. M. 123

Sells, M. A. 37
Serbian 24, 80, 90–102, 110
Shapiro, E. xviii
shared targets 25–27
Sharon, A. 106–108
Silberstein, O. 46
Sinhalese 30, 63
Slovakia 4
Smith, D. L. 29
Smith, J. 105
Smith, J. H. 68
Snidal, D. 2
Sokollu Mehmed Pasha 92, 100
Solyom, A. E. 22
South Africa 29, 79–80
South Ossetians xvii, 20, 50–51, 72–74
Soviets xviii, 2, 4, 95, 118
Soviet Union 2, 4, 50, 64, 72, 95, 122
Spitz, R. 25
splitting 59, 61
    defensive 84
    developmental 84
Sri Lanka 63
Stalin, J. 82
Stambolić, I. 98
Stefan Dušan, Emperor 89–90
Stefan Lazarević 90
Stein, H. 29
Stein, J. G. 2
Steinberg, B. 86
Stern, D. N. 19, 83
Stern, J. 64
Stiglitz, J. E. 123
Stokes, P. 5
suicide bombers xiv, 114–118
survival guilt 23
Swift, E. M. 79–80

Tähkä, V. 66
Tamils 30, 63
Tatars 24
Tate, C. 10

terrorism xiii, xv, 8, 15, 46, 48, 81,
    114–115, 117, 122–123
terrorists 5, 46, 60, 114, 117–118
Thompson, K. W. 34
time collapse 31, 41, 76, 96–101,
    109–110
totalitarian objects 61
track two diplomacy 15
transgenerational transmission xix,
    5, 22, 25, 45, 57–58, 71, 91, 102
Transylvania 20
trauma xii, xiv, xix, 4–5, 8–9, 23–24,
    35–36, 40, 43, , 59, 63, 67, 71, 83,
    96, 102–103, 109, 115
Tree Model 125, 127
Tsarnaev, D. 119
Tsarnaev, T. 119
Tucker, R. C. 82
Turkey xii, xviii, 3–4, 21, 31, 34–35,
    41, 46–48, 61
Turks xviii, 10, 24, 26, 35–36, 39–40,
    61, 90–91, 98, 100, 117
    Cypriot 43, 48–49
Tutu, D. xviii

Varvin, S. 5
Vasquez 12, 34
victimisation 8, 23, 50, 73, 80, 91, 93,
    95, 101, 109–110
Volkan, K. 75
Volkan, V. D. xii–xvi, 3–5, 21–22, 24,
    27, 34–35, 39–41, 46–48, 50–51, 55,
    60–62, 66, 69–72, 74–75, 79, 81,
    83–86, 92, 96, 113–114, 122–123,
    125
von Rochau, L. 1
Vulliamy, E. 95–96, 98

Waco xii
Waelder, R. 6, 24, 60
war(s) ix–xi, xiii, xv, 6, 8–9, 14, 21, 35,
    42, 46–48, 57, 64, 81, 122

Balkan 35, 93–94
Boer 79
Bosnian 101
Cambodia civil 88
Cold 2
Georgian-South Ossetian 20,
   50–51, 72
Greek War of Independence 42
Gulf 61
Israel–Syria 107
Muslim holy 12
Operation Just Cause
Vietnam 74, 86
World War I x–xi, 11, 35, 94, 112
World War II 1, 96, 105, 107,
   111–114
Yom Kippur 2
Watts, D. P. 28
Weber, M. 79
Weigert, E. 83
Weimar Republic 5
West Bank xviii, 115
Williams, R. M. 47
Wills, G. 105
Winnicott, D. W. 70
Wolfenstein, M. 45, 67

World Health Organization (WHO)
   57
Worthington, E. 124
Wounded Knee 24

United Kingdom xviii, 195
United Nations High Commissioner
   for Refugees (UNHCR) 57
United States xviii, 1–2, 4–5, 13, 24,
   26–27, 29, 33, 40–41, 60, 62, 74, 88,
   100, 105, 113, 118
   African Americans 5, 29
   Americans xviii, 2, 7, 74
   Japanese Americans 23
University of Virginia xviii, 4, 72, 99

Yitzak Rabin Center for Israeli
   Studies 62, 104–105, 107
Yosef, O. 106
Young, K. 40
Yugoslavia 29, 55, 64, 80–81, 94–96,
   99, 101, 109

Zamblios, S. 42
Zintl, E. 66, 69

For Product Safety Concerns and Information please contact our EU
representative GPSR@taylorandfrancis.com
Taylor & Francis Verlag GmbH, Kaufingerstraße 24, 80331 München, Germany

www.ingramcontent.com/pod-product-compliance
Lightning Source LLC
Chambersburg PA
CBHW062035270326
41929CB00014B/2435